INTERMEDIATE

# How to Pass
## Advanced
## Aptitude Tests

Assess your potential and analyse your career options with graduate and managerial level psychometric tests

2nd edition

Jim Barrett

**KoganPage**

LONDON PHILADELPHIA NEW DELHI

First published in 2002
Revised edition 2008
Second edition 2010

120 Pentonville Road
London N1 9JN
United Kingdom
www.koganpage.com

525 South 4th Street, #241
Philadelphia PA 19147
USA

4737/23 Ansari Road
Daryaganj
New Delhi 110002
India

© Jim Barrett, 2002, 2008, 2010

The right of Jim Barrett to be identified as the author of this work has been asserted by him in accordance with the Copyright, Designs and Patents Act 1988.

ISBN      978 0 7494 6142 3
E-ISBN   978 0 7494 5428 9

**British Library Cataloguing in Publication Data**

A CIP record for this book is available from the British Library.

**Library of Congress Cataloging-in-Publication data**

Barrett, Jim.
   How to pass advanced aptitude tests : assess your potential and analyse your career options with graduate and managerial level psychometric tests / Jim Barrett. – 2nd ed.
      p. cm.
   Includes bibliographical references and index.
   ISBN 978-0-7494-6142-3 – ISBN 978-0-7494-5428-9   1. Occupational aptitude tests. 2. Vocational interests–Testing.   3. Ability–Testing.   I. Title.
   HF5381.7.B37 2010
   153.9′4–dc22
                                                                        2010019257

Typeset by Graphicraft Limited, Hong Kong
Printed and bound in India by Replika Press Pvt Ltd

# How to Pass
## Advanced
## Aptitude Tests

# Contents

# Preface

The significant addition to this new edition is the Extrapolation Test, which replaces the Organizational Skills Test. Whilst both tests require power of concentration, the Organizational Skills Test did not sufficiently challenge the intellectual fluidity that is often the key aptitude necessary for 'high level executive decision making'. The Extrapolation Test assesses the essential conceptual demands of abstract distillation frequently required in careers at a senior level. The standard of all the tests in this volume is at a level readers may well encounter, for example, for university 'thinking skills' tests, for entry to business school and other advanced, high-level assessment programmes.

# Introduction: How to Succeed with Tests

You can use the tests in this book for practice and guidance. You will get the most from them if you understand why tests have become so important as:

- aids to selection and development;
- assessment methods for educational and training courses;
- measures for occupational placement and development.

The Introduction intends to provide some background information about psychological, sometimes called 'psychometric', testing, its purposes and how it works. At the very least, it is advisable to read thoroughly the notes contained within this Introduction relating to 'How to approach tests' before you embark upon the tests in Part 1 of this book.

## Purpose of this book

In this book you have access to tests of a type used by educational and business organizations for purposes of selection, recruitment and development. By 'test' is meant both timed tests of aptitude and ability as well as untimed questionnaires, unless these are referred to separately in the text. These types of test are commonly referred to as 'psychometric' tests. 'Psychometric' means, literally, 'to measure an aspect of the mind'. It is a standard way, that is, a scientific way of measuring what a person can do or how he or she behaves. How tests do this is discussed later in the text. The two major aims of the book are: 1) to provide an opportunity to become familiar with tests in order to perform optimally in 'real' test situations; 2) to offer guidance based upon test results.

Most organizations now prefer to use tests than rely upon public examination results as these often seem to have little relevance to what is required when actually doing a job. Instead, job-related tests have been specifically designed to assess characteristics that predict likely competence in a job function, whether these are mental or physical skills, personal or social accomplishments. This is exactly what was predicted more than 20 years ago in *Test Your Own Aptitude* and in my later books, *Career, Aptitude and Selection Tests* and *Aptitude, Personality and Motivation Tests* (see Bibliography). Practice on the tests in this book can prepare you for similar tests that you may well encounter in your life. The following are some of the typical and routine situations in which tests are now used:

- as a complement to an interview as part of a job application;
- degree, professional or other training course application;
- career promotion;
- career development review;
- assessment centre programme.

So, it is wise to increase your awareness of what is required in such situations. Being prepared, you will be able to respond with confidence and give a true and accurate picture of yourself.

This book may also assist you to evaluate the career or careers that suit you best. For those people in a career already, it may be able to suggest lines of career management and opportunity without necessarily going through any trauma that might be involved in attempting to 'turn the clock back'; career fulfilment often has more to do with a qualitative adjustment or refocusing of a career as opposed to making a radical change between different fields of work.

This volume follows in the sound footsteps of *Test Your Own Aptitude*, whose purpose was to provide a structured means of discovering hidden potential. It was directed primarily towards school leavers, although people of all ages found it to be a useful guide to career review and possibly career change. With equal effect the present volume is applicable to people searching for a career or career adjustment when those taking the tests anticipate being in, or are already engaged in, a career at a managerial, professional or graduate level. For this reason the tests in this volume are raised in difficulty and permit extra scope for evaluation.

Owing to the unique characteristics of those who might take the tests in this book, it is not possible to provide a definitive solution to the job search of any individual. Whilst in many cases it will no doubt be found to provide an accurate evaluation and a clear guide, the intention is more modest: taking into account the multifarious differences that exist between people, this book intends to do no more than provide a structured approach to assess how your characteristics may relate to different types of work activity. This is no more than the well-known process of attempting to ensure that 'round pegs' do not go into 'square holes', but with the insight that arises from employing well-used psychological methods that have been devised in an attempt to obtain the best 'job fit'. Tests can do this by:

- looking at potential in a similar way for everybody;

- attempting to 'take stock' of talent that may be affected, contaminated and distorted by so many other variables, in particular, educational disadvantage or prejudice;

- trying to ensure that there is some opportunity for people to demonstrate the resources they have.

# The advantages and limitations of a test

All of us are testing everything and everybody we encounter every day. We make judgements, usually on the basis of our experience. If we did not have experience as a measuring device to help us, we would proceed haphazardly from one experience to the next. Sometimes we might doubt our experience or have insufficient of it. Tests are another form of measuring device that can add to our experience, thereby enabling us to make more informed choices. In this case we are seeking a basis to check whether our assumptions are correct and to extend our knowledge. In so far as those people to whom you are applying for a position, job vacancy or training programme are concerned, they may have very little experience of you, and they may take your curriculum vitae or your examination results with a pinch of salt! Even if they do know you because you have been working for them for a while, they may still be unsure as to whether you could manage a more difficult or different job. Therefore, they may well want to learn more about you by using the quick, objective and relevant means of testing.

Tests allow us to overcome our prejudices and subjective impressions. The trouble with relying on our intuition is that two people comparing the same thing may have contrary experiences. One person says, 'I thought she was very clever', whilst another says, 'Really I thought she was not', or one says, 'I thought he was very well organized', to which the other replies, 'Well, he never gave me the message he was supposed to pass to me.' I remember my father, who was a cavalry officer, saying, 'You can always tell a man by his shoes.' A business lady I once met stated that she always rejected a handwritten curriculum vitae (CV), but other business leaders ask for a CV to be handwritten. Prejudicial judgements are insoluble to a candidate because they have no way of knowing what they are being measured against. Tests that measure mental reasoning, behaviour or motivation, like any other scientific measure, say of height or weight, are designed to give us all the same information so that we all know what we are talking about. They enable us to state, with a certain confidence, 'how much' of a certain characteristic or 'how likely' certain events might be.

## Reliability and validity

It is the capacity to measure the same characteristic in the same way that makes a test a 'reliable' measure. Reliability, that is, something we can predict will always work the same way, is essential in order that we can obtain 'valid' information about ourselves. By 'valid' is meant that the information is sound enough for us to make decisions that are better than chance. Obviously, if a test has no validity there is little point in using it, unless our purpose is merely to have fun! This is why so little notice is taken of horoscopes, palm reading, crystal ball gazing and similar activities. Therefore, tests are just like any other tools that may increase efficiency and hence productivity in an organization. How well the test works, that is, how reliable is the result, also depends upon you! To the extent you are underprepared for the test and, therefore, could have done better, the test will not measure you accurately and you will have let yourself down unnecessarily.

If your intention is to gain familiarity with different types of tests, but you are not concerned with what your level of performance, attainment or 'score' might mean, then you will probably not be interested in whether the test is an accurate measure of anything. But if you would like to obtain some guidance from the tests in this book, you will want to have some idea of:

- what you are best at;
- how you compare with other people;
- how your results might relate to different occupations.

## 'Differential' tests

The comparative processes above are possible only if the tests are able to measure your talents and those of others in the same way.

In other words, the tests will be measuring 'like with like'. This is particularly important with tests such as those in Part 1, which are tests of mental measurement and where relative aptitude on the different tests may be a significant factor in career guidance. The tests in this book are of a special kind termed '*differential*' tests because they can say whether a person's performance on one test really is greater than that on another test. Example tests of this power that are widely used by psychologists are: the 'General Ability Tests', published by The Morrisby Organization, and 'The Differential Aptitude Test Battery', published by Psychological Corporation Ltd. The essential characteristic of differential tests is that each test measures a different aptitude and then compares the result on one test with a result on another. As the tests are developed they are compared with each other to make sure that they really are measuring different mental aspects. This is a statistical exercise called *test correlation*. None of the tests in this book correlate with each other very much, so all are measuring an aspect of intelligence that is different from the others. To ensure this is the case the tests have had to be developed with people who have each taken all of the tests. It is this process that makes each test useful as a single test, but even more powerful as '*differential*' tests.

However, the tests have not been tried out on sufficient numbers of people or, indeed, sufficient distinct groups or types of people to be able to provide definitive solutions. Whilst the tests in this book can suggest some ideas or possibilities about yourself that you may want to pursue, you can seek further advice from a psychologist, who will administer reliable tests that are relevant to your particular situation, age group and background. They will provide you with a much more valid result than is possible within the confines of this book. (It is possible to consult organizations providing career guidance. If you do so, make sure that you will be given a complete battery of tests, including aptitude tests, and that you will have access to a properly qualified psychologist.)

## The 'average' and 'standard deviation'

In the meantime, whilst the tests in this volume do not claim to be able to give you precise information and guidance in your individual case, but only to give you a sound structure through which to analyse your potential, they have been pretested many times to ensure that they are some measure of what is intended. They have been tried out on many people with various backgrounds and with various qualifications ranging in age from 16 to 60 years. When the results of many people are collected together it is useful to find an 'average' and then have a way of finding out how far any one person is different, or deviates, from the 'average'. Statisticians call the average a '*mean*' and the difference a '*standard deviation*' or 'SD'. The 'average' will be a familiar concept to you, whilst the 'SD' may not be. The SD is used by statisticians as well as by psychologists. It is a figure that is based upon the 'average' of all the people within a certain group who have taken the tests. It tells how far any individual score is different from (or 'deviates' from) the average of the group. If you have a score that is one SD above the average, you are roughly doing better than 70 per cent of the group. If you have a score that is two SDs above the average, you are roughly doing better than 95 per cent of the group. For those who are interested in the characteristics of the aptitude tests used here, the statistics, in round numbers, are as follows:

| Test | 1<br>Vis. | 2<br>Num. | 3<br>Verb. | 4<br>Form | 5<br>Ext. | 6<br>Tech. | 7<br>Analyt. |
|------|------|------|------|------|------|------|------|
| Mean | 22 | 10 | 19 | 14 | 7 | 10 | 10 |
| SD | 7 | 5 | 6 | 8 | 2 | 5 | 5 |

## Interpreting your test score

So, if in the Visual Logic test, you obtained a score of 29, your score would be one SD above the mean or average. Psychologists know that you are therefore performing at a level above that of approximately 70 per cent of other people who have done the test. If your score was 36, then you would have performed better than approximately 95 per cent of other people on this test. So, the greater your SD, the more likely it is that your aptitude really is greater or less than other people.

Similarly, it is possible to compare your performances on two or more different tests. For example, if your score was around the mean on one test, but around one SD higher on another test, this would give you reasonable cause to think that you really were better on one type of problem solving than another and, further, that this finding might give you cause to consider what this imbalance in your aptitudes on these tests might mean for the type of work you would be best at. Again, the greater the differences in your performances on these tests, the stronger the evidence is likely to be.

In both the above illustrations, care must be taken not to take the results too literally, but only as indications. This is because the tests may not be measuring you precisely, again because of testing conditions or because the tests themselves are not precise enough or because many other factors about you need to be taken into account. There are many ways in which your score on any test might be inaccurate or indicate 'under-attainment'. Presuming the tests were administered in the correct conditions, psychologists have ways of calculating how likely it is that your score has a degree of *measurement error* and this needs to be taken into account before it is possible to say just how good you really are on any test. This is intended only to give you an indication of what is involved in trying to estimate your potential. Further explanation of the statistics of test measurement is beyond the scope of this book. Other tests you will encounter in 'real' test situations will provide you with more accurate results because they will apply the necessary statistical processes more precisely to tests that are reliable and valid for the circumstances in which you are taking them.

## Standardization

A psychometric test, such as the ones in this book, is one that aims to measure psychological characteristics that are expressed through different actions. These tests are 'standardized', which means that they have characteristics that anybody can understand if they want to, in the same way that everybody can feel how heavy a kilo is or see how long a metre is. Thus, they are measuring instruments because they permit some basis upon which comparison can be made. Unless it is known what the 'measure' actually is, it will be impossible to compare one person's performance against that of another so that you will be able to say with some level of accuracy how much a result is above or below average. Therefore, what 'average' actually means becomes crucial. For the tests in Part 1 of this book 'average' is approximately between a 'D' and 'C', approximating to most people. 'C' is above average, whilst 'B' is well above average, approximating to people who have the potential to go on to higher education and to people who have obtained a higher qualification. A score of 'A' is very high indeed, giving exceptional evidence of aptitude in this area. Your score on a test is called a *'raw score'*. This is the number you got correct. The raw score makes no sense until you compare it with a *'standardized'* score. In this case the standard scores range from F to A. In the section How to Interpret and Apply Your Aptitudes you can enter your raw score in the chart and find your equivalent standard score.

## Correlation

A score on a test will only make sense if it can be rated against something else. What the test actually means in practical terms is what you will want to know. This is often the limitation of tests that merely provide a measure of intelligence, 'intelligence quotient' or 'IQ' tests, because they may not tell us much about what a person can actually do in real terms. Aptitude tests are designed to provide more practical, usable information. Thus, how effectively your 'measure' can predict how well people will succeed in other, different activities is another statistical process called 'correlation'. It is a measure of how well we can be certain that the presence of one thing predicts that something else is likely to happen. For example, how well would a high score on the test of Numerical Insight predict that a person could qualify as a mathematician or how well would a high score on the Technical test predict that a person could qualify as an engineer? The answers in both cases are that the tests give an indication, but do not predict those possible events with certainty because they have not been researched exhaustively enough to be a scientific correlation. When you think about it, there are too many other factors to be taken account of, such as what other talents does the person possess, are they interested in pursuing their talent, do their circumstances allow them to follow that direction, as well as how well the test is assessing a key talent that is required in a particular job. And when you take into account the fact that different organizations may require different aspects of that talent or for that talent to be combined with others, the number of 'variables' becomes far too many to deal with in a book. To do so, it would be necessary to correlate all the tests in this book with the six hundred or so careers that are given in the Occupational Index, an impossible task.

Therefore, the relationship between test performance and careers is based upon my own experience of using tests in career guidance with many thousands of people of all ages. I hope that you will find that my experience has some validity for you. No doubt many readers will find themselves in a testing situation in which the attributes that are being assessed have been exhaustively researched in order that they produce a scientific correlation with the job for which they are applying. However, tests are often used merely as general guides or as schemes or checklists to facilitate an interview, particularly in the case of personality and career type tests.

If you want to receive accurate, standardized information about your intellectual or other potential, you would need to be properly assessed by a psychologist in order that:

1  the tests are administered in conditions that will produce an accurate result;

2  the results are interpreted properly;

3  the results are compared specifically against a relevant group; and

4  the results are compared against specific criteria, such as measured skill needed for success on a specific course of training or in a particular job.

# How to approach tests

You will obtain most from the tests in this book if you read the notes on guidance on how to take tests, below, and also follow exactly the instructions preceding each test. A test will not tell us anything very much unless taken in the optimum conditions. Therefore, you must ensure that the conditions in which you take tests allow you to do your best. The tests may be online or you may be asked to sit a paper-and-pen version. Here is a checklist covering testing situations in general:

● You must not be distracted. Ensure that you will not be interrupted by other people or sounds that might intrude.

● You must be comfortable. If you are too hot or cold or other things put you off, such as poor lighting, then let someone know. If you want to take time out to go to the lavatory, then it is sensible to say so.

● Be prepared. Before attending the test session make sure that you have covered any options such as pre-reading, that there are no exercises that it is impossible for you to do, that you have asked what you should bring, how long the process will take and what it will consist of.

- Read the instructions. Do this thoroughly, taking as much time as you require. Do not be intimidated if other people being tested at the same time as yourself seem to have finished – the important thing in your case is that you should be clear as to exactly what is expected of you.

- Work through the examples. Do this thoroughly as well. If there is something you do not understand, make sure you do understand it before you start the test itself. You can take as much time as you want before starting a test.

- Anything else. A properly trained test invigilator will be on the alert to assist you with any difficulty. They will encourage you to mention anything that might be an issue before the test as well as after it. If something has occurred to you during the test you should mention it, because it might be of sufficient importance to be taken into account when the test is marked and interpreted.

The example that follows is similar to the instructions that you might be given when taking tests in formal situations. They are given at length here in order to provide you with full information and as a means of substituting for instructions that you will not be receiving as you take the tests in this book by yourself. If it is a paper-and-pen test, the test administrator (someone who has been trained to administer tests properly) may say something like:

You have pencils and rough paper in front of you. If you want more, please let me know. I will give out the test in a moment.

You will now be asked to complete a series of timed aptitude tests. You will be told when to start and when to stop. You will be given plenty of time to read the instructions and do some practice examples before you start each test. It is important that you understand what is expected of you before you start. It is necessary to work quickly on the tests. The tests are very short and there is no time to keep looking at your own watch. Simply work as quickly as you can, but do not rush on so quickly that you feel you may be making mistakes. Go as fast as you can but try to make sure that what you are doing is correct. Try not to guess as that may count against you.

You will probably find that there are too many items for you to complete within the time given. The tests are designed this way. You are not expected to get to the end of the test in the time given, but to get as many answers correct as you can.

Do not turn over until you are told. Write your name and other details on the front page. Then read the instructions. If there are any examples you should do them. You can do any working out you want to on the booklet and inside the booklet when you are told to turn over. You are also given some paper for rough working.

When completing the answer sheet, you must make it clear what your answer is. If you want to change your answer, rub it out completely and fill in the answer you prefer, so there is no doubt which is the correct one.

When you have read the instructions and tried out the examples please ask any questions. Wait to be given the instruction to turn over.

## Guessing

The whole point of a test is that someone will come across many items where they cannot be absolutely certain, and even if they are absolutely certain in their own mind, they may nevertheless be wrong. Guessing is therefore inevitable, but what you want to eliminate is wild guessing, because this will not improve your score and might well reduce it. However, in the case of individual items where you think you probably know the answer, although you are not absolutely sure, it is probably worthwhile making a choice rather than leaving the item out. This is particularly the case in tests where the answer cannot be exactly quantified, as in numerical tests, but could be evaluative or interpretative, for example, with verbal concepts.

What should you do if you get stuck on an item? With aptitude tests that are designed to get more difficult as you go through them, if you get stuck on an item it may be best to leave it and go on to the next. Although the next item may well be slightly more difficult you will probably be able to do it once you 'free yourself up' from an item on which your concentration may just temporarily have given up.

# PART ONE

# Aptitudes

# Introduction

The following remarks, whilst directed towards the tests in this book, are also intended as general advice for tests you might take in 'real' test situations where you may not be able to find out beforehand what tests you might be given. Therefore, this book prepares you for tests you might encounter. Some you are going to do are abstract and some are practical. Some, such as the Verbal Concepts test, because of vocabulary depend to a large extent upon abilities you have learnt beforehand. If the results on these tests show you to be relatively weak, you can improve your performance by giving yourself some practice. Others, like the Visual Logic test or the Form Recognition test, are of a type that is not so dependent upon prior knowledge. Some of these tests are looking for flexibility, perceptiveness or insight in your reasoning. For example, it is not for nothing that the Numerical Insight test contains the word 'insight'. This test, like other 'reasoning' tests, gives you a hint that the test may be searching for something deeper than the ability to add numbers. In this case, it is the potential to perceive the connections between numbers in sometimes different, new ways. Therefore, the key overall rule for you to follow is that, having read the instructions and done the examples to a test, you should be clear about what the test is going to demand of you before you start it.

## 1.   Problems 'on your mind'

If something has happened to you that is absorbing your attention it is better to take the tests when you are in a more settled frame of mind. Such matters may be lack of sleep, poor health, or worry about other people. (In a real test situation any such matter should be reported as soon as possible. It is then the responsibility of the person testing you to decide whether they are able to make allowance for your circumstances in the test results or whether any results might be worthless in those circumstances. After all, they want to obtain an accurate picture, otherwise they will be wasting their time.)

## 2.  Preparation

Check that you have everything you need before you start the test. If it is a paper-and-pen test, have you sufficient pencils? Have you an eraser? Have you got spare paper? Is there anything that might 'put you off' or disturb you?

## 3.  Reading instructions

Always make sure you are absolutely certain what you have to do before you start. The tests are strictly timed and you will lose out if you have to stop, go back and reread the explanation (or ask for assistance from an invigilator in a real test situation).

## 4.  Do not have preconceptions about how well you might do

You may think you are going to perform better on some tests than others. You may like some tests better than others. These thoughts will be based upon your past experience, but have little relationship to what you can actually do. Therefore, try your utmost on all the tests, as you may be better on some tests than you expect.

## 5.  Read the explanation carefully

Do any examples and make sure you understand any explanation. (If you are in a real test situation where you are being tested along-side others, do not feel rushed into starting before you are ready just because you do not want to look stupid. If you ask for an explan-ation, the chances are that others will also be glad to have an explan-ation of the same thing!)

## 6.  Timing

Most of the tests in this book are too long for you to complete in the time given. They are designed that way. Therefore, do not begin to rush if you think that time must be running out. Work at a speed at which you feel you are in control and are not having to guess. (In a real test situation, where there may be other candidates, do not be put off by a candidate who seems to be working very quickly. They might be leaving items out or they might be getting what they do wrong. If you are unsure, ask the invigilator if you should have a watch or clock to refer to. You can also ask whether it is possible to be given a warning that you have a certain amount of time left before the end of the test.)

# 7.   Guessing

This is generally a waste of time because you are missing an opportunity to get something right. Also, having spent time on working on an item, you lose that time if you throw it away with random guessing. If you have a strong 'hunch' that you know the answer, it is better to make a choice than nothing at all, but if you do this too many times, your guessing will count against you. If you are 'stuck' on an item it is better to leave it and go on to the next as you will at least avoid getting a wrong answer, whilst also giving yourself the option to come back to that item later.

# 8.   Marking the answer paper

Make sure your answer is clear, otherwise you will not get a score. On some tests you are only required to count the number of answers you have got correct. On others you have to make a correction. For example, you may have to take a quarter of those you have got wrong away from the number you have got correct. In this case, take the number you have wrong to the lowest whole number, so that if you got 5 wrong you would take one mark away from your score, whereas 7 wrong would mean that you take two marks away from your score, and 13 wrong would mean you take three marks from the number you had correct, and so on.

## 9.   Drawing on the answer paper

In a paper-and-pen test, do not worry about making marks, drawings or doing calculations on the page of tests (unless this is not your copy!). What is required is the correct answer, so tidiness is unimportant. Many people prefer to make jottings on the answer sheet itself rather than use spare paper, and this is perfectly acceptable and is not cheating! If you need to make a note or do a sum, it is often quicker to do any rough work in the margin than switch to spare paper. This is certainly true of the Analytical test, where it is helpful if you actually draw the figures as you work out the answer rather than try to hold all the information in your head. At the same time, you must not spoil test papers that may have to be used again by others. Always ensure you have sufficient rough paper. (In a real test situation you may be given a separate answer sheet and question booklet. The former is usually disposable once used, the second is usually expensive and will be used many times, so ruining this will not endear you to others, though the invigilator should have made sure that you were fully aware and kept to any such rule relating to the preservation of test papers.)

## 10.   Be aware of your situation

In a real test situation, make sure that the invigilator is aware of conflicts or difficulties that may affect your performance. This might be something that happened during testing – for example, you realized at the end there was another sheet you had missed, you broke all your pencils and had to wait, and so on – or outside factors – for example, you are 'jet-lagged', you have a cold, you are worried about the health of a relative, and so on.

# Test 1 Visual Logic

This is a test of how well you perceive how lines and shapes are connected. You are given a question and some alternative drawings. You have to choose the one drawing that is the most logical.

You can mark your answer on the page in the way that suits you best. You can cross the correct answer through, mark with a tick, circle or underline. It is best to mark your answer with a pencil so that you can erase it if you change your mind. The first of the examples below has been done already.

**Examples**

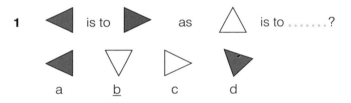

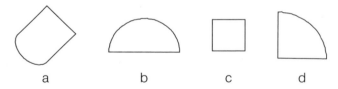

In the first example alternative 'b' is the answer as it is exactly the opposite. In the second example alternative 'c' is the only drawing without a curve.

This test lasts 15 minutes. You have to work accurately and do as many questions as you can in the time allowed. When you are ready, start the test that begins over the page and start your timer as you do so. Keep going until you have finished the last question or run out of time.

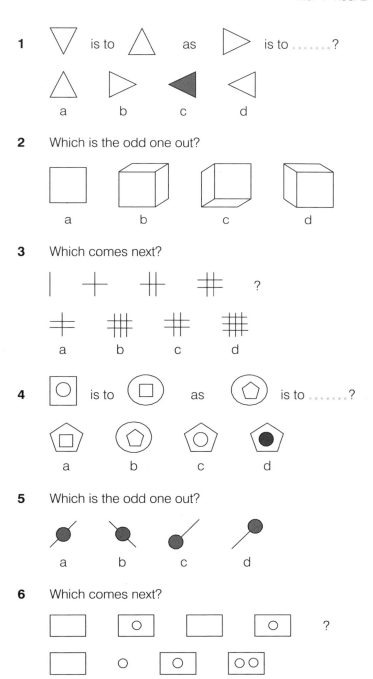

**1**  ▽ is to △ as ▷ is to ........?

a  b  c  d

**2**  Which is the odd one out?

a  b  c  d

**3**  Which comes next?

? 

a  b  c  d

**4**  ⊡ is to ◯□ as ◯⬠ is to ........?

a  b  c  d

**5**  Which is the odd one out?

a  b  c  d

**6**  Which comes next?

?

a  b  c  d

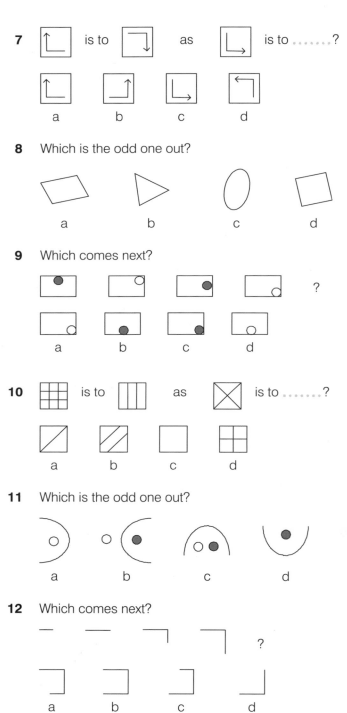

**7** ... is to ... as ... is to .......?

a    b    c    d

**8**  Which is the odd one out?

a    b    c    d

**9**  Which comes next?

?

a    b    c    d

**10** ... is to ... as ... is to .......?

a    b    c    d

**11** Which is the odd one out?

a    b    c    d

**12** Which comes next?

?

a    b    c    d

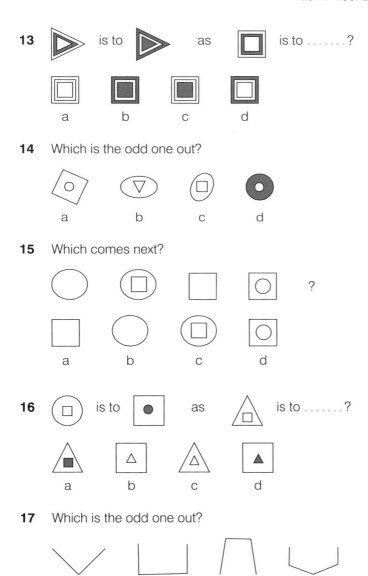

**13**    is to    as    is to ........?

a    b    c    d

**14**    Which is the odd one out?

a    b    c    d

**15**    Which comes next?

?

a    b    c    d

**16**    is to    as    is to ........?

a    b    c    d

**17**    Which is the odd one out?

a    b    c    d

**18** Which comes next?

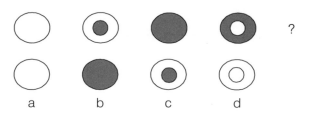

    a        b        c        d

**19**

    a        b        c        d

**20** Which is the odd one out?

    a        b        c        d

**21** Which comes next?

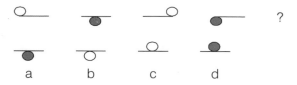

    a        b        c        d

**22** ☐▷ is to ☐◀ as ☐▽ is to ........?

    a        b        c        d

**23**    Which is the odd one out?

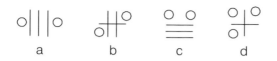

**24**    Which comes next?

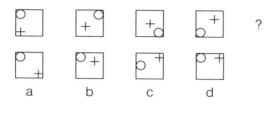

**25**

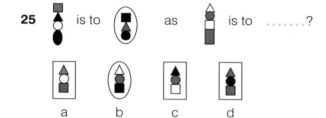

**26**    Which is the odd one out?

**27**    Which comes next?

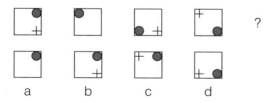

**28**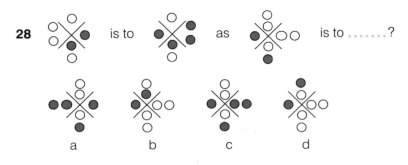

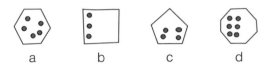

a b c d

**29** Which is the odd one out?

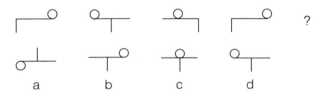

a b c d

**30** Which comes next?

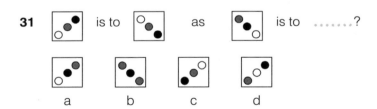

a b c d

**31**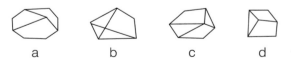

a b c d

**32** Which is the odd one out?

**33**   Which comes next?

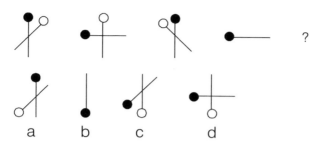

?

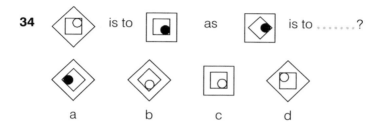

a          b          c          d

**34**

is to ........?

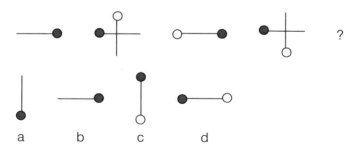

a            b            c            d

**35**   Which is the odd one out?

a            b            c            d

**36**   Which comes next?

?

a            b            c            d

**37**   Which is the odd one out?

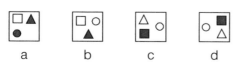

a            b            c            d

**38**   Which comes next?

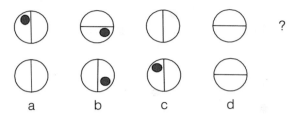

**39**   Which is the odd one out?

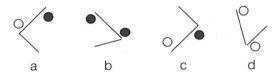

# Answers to Test 1

| | | | | | | | |
|---|---|---|---|---|---|---|---|
| **1** | d | **11** | b | **21** | c | **31** | a |
| **2** | a | **12** | a | **22** | b | **32** | b |
| **3** | b | **13** | b | **23** | d | **33** | a |
| **4** | c | **14** | d | **24** | d | **34** | b |
| **5** | b | **15** | b | **25** | a | **35** | b |
| **6** | a | **16** | d | **26** | a | **36** | b |
| **7** | d | **17** | c | **27** | b | **37** | a |
| **8** | c | **18** | a | **28** | a | **38** | c |
| **9** | b | **19** | c | **29** | d | **39** | d |
| **10** | a | **20** | a | **30** | d | | |

RAW SCORE = Number of correct answers minus ¼ of incorrect answers.

GRADES

| | |
|---|---|
| A score of 32 or over | grade A |
| 26–31 | grade B |
| 20–25 | grade C |
| 15–19 | grade D |
| 10–14 | grade E |
| 0–9 | grade F |

Transfer your grade to the chart on page 94.

# Explanations to Test 1

## *Visual Logic*

1    In the example, the triangle has been 'flipped', pointing up and then down. The answer could only be 'a' if the original triangles had been rotated by 90 degrees, not by 180 degrees. 'B' reflects the triangle vertically, but is not satisfactory as it is the same image as the original triangle. There is no reason provided by the example pair why the answer should be a

shaded triangle, so 'c' is unsatisfactory. The answer is 'd' because it has been 'flipped' in just the same way as the example, albeit horizontally as opposed to vertically.

**2**    Only answer 'a' is of a figure that is not three dimensional.

**3**    The sequence is 1, 2, 3 and 4 lines, so next would be 5 lines.

**4**    The rule is that the outside figure becomes the inside figure.

**5**    The figure for answer 'b' has a different orientation from the others.

**6**    The figures are repeated in a chain so that a rectangle is followed by a circle in a rectangle. The next figure will be a rectangle; answer 'a'. All of the other answers would break the pattern.

**7**    In the example, the figure has been rotated 180 degrees or, alternatively, has been 'flipped' and has been given a 'mirror image'. 'D' is the answer that has gone through the same process.

**8**    All the figures apart from 'c' have straight sides.

**9**    The next figure must be a rectangle, and within this must be a black circle, not a white circle, which would break the pattern. White circles appear to move successively clockwise from corner to corner of the rectangle, whilst black circles appear to move successively clockwise from side to side, so the answer is 'b'.

**10**    Half the number of lines in the original figure are removed in each case.

**11**    Only in answer 'b' is there a circle outside the curve.

**12**    The first line is half the length of the second line. The third line, which is attached to the second line, goes downwards and is half the length of the fourth line. The expectation is that the fifth figure would be another 'half' line. There is no evidence that the resulting figure should be 'flipped' (as in answer 'c'), so the correct answer is 'a'.

**13**    In the first drawing, a white triangle is placed 'on top of' a black triangle, which is itself placed on top of a white triangle. This is equivalent to the second drawing, in which the top triangle is black, then white, then black. The same pattern or sequence follows with the square drawings.

**14**  'D' is the only answer than contains two figures of the same shape.

**15**  The first figure is plain and a circle. The second figure has a square inside the circle. In the third figure the square has covered the circle and has become, like the first figure, a plain one. In the fourth figure a circle has appeared in the square. The progression is of plain figures, then figures containing a smaller figure, which then becomes the next plain figure, so the answer is 'b'.

**16**  The circle frames the square, which then becomes the outside figure, whilst the circle becomes shaded. Therefore, the square should become the outside figure, whilst the triangle becomes the inside, shaded figure; answer 'd'.

**17**  Answer 'c' is the only figure that 'opens' downwards.
(NOTE: with these sorts of problems, other answers often contain possibilities that are also 'odd' but are, when you think carefully, not 'odd' enough. For example, answer 'a' is the only one to have two lines and 'd' is the only one to have four. So, why should either of these answers be better than the other? Again, only 'b' has a figure with a base at the bottom, but why should this be more 'odd' than figure 'c', which has a 'base' at the top? To solve these sorts of problems it is necessary to find the answer for which no other answer has an equivalent or complementary feature).

**18**  White alternates with black, so the next figure will be plain white. The order is therefore as follows: a white circle, a black circle within the white circle, a black circle covering the white circle so that it is all black, a white circle appearing in the black circle, then, finally, the inner white circle will cover the black circle so that it is all white; answer 'a'.

**19**  In the example, the triangle is removed and the circle becomes black. Therefore, if the pentagon is removed, the outside square should remain the same and the inner square should become black; answer 'c'.

**20**  In answer 'a' the 'arms' of the inner figure are turned 'inwards' within the larger figure, whereas all three of the other figures remain entirely 'open'.

**21**   As white and black circles appear in sequence, a white ball should be next, so the answer is 'b' or 'c'. There is no reason why the white ball should be under the line since the sequence seems to be over, under, over, under. So the next figure should be a white ball above the line; answer 'c'.

**22**   The small, white triangle becomes a black triangle that has been reversed or flipped 180 degrees. We should expect the white triangle to become a black triangle again reversed. 'B' is the only satisfactory answer.

**23**   All but 'd' have three lines and two circles.

**24**   The white circle moves successively clockwise to the next corner of the square so that it will next appear in the top left hand corner. The cross moves across the square so that it will next appear at the top right of the square. Both these positions are covered by answer 'd'.

**25**   In the first example, the lowest, oval figure of the set disappears. Its colour, black, becomes the colour of the square in the second set. The colours are transmitted down from one small figure to the next in each set. So, the shaded square becomes black, the black triangle becomes shaded and the white circle becomes black. Thus, we would expect the third set to go from white triangle to shaded, shaded circle to white and white square to shaded; answer 'a'.

**26**   Only 'a' has a line that does not join corners.

**27**   Whilst the black circle moves successively anticlockwise from corner to corner, the cross moves successively from bottom right to top left of the square.

**28**   One set mirrors the other set whilst the two white circles are changed to two black circles along the horizontal.

**29**   Only 'd' has more small circles than the number of sides of the figure within which they appear.

**30**   The circle moves on top of the line and from its right to its left end, then moves back to the halfway point, then to the right again, so the next move is most likely to be again at the left end. The small, vertical line goes from extreme left, to middle, to the right and then to again to the left. So the next move is likely to be to the middle. It seems that both the circle and the vertical line only move to the middle of the horizontal line in one direction and that this is a different direction.

**31** The first pair is a vertical mirror image, whilst the second pair is a horizontal mirror image. Alternatively, the three inner figures move around the inner square clockwise from corner to corner.

**32** Only 'b' has two lines that bisect each other.

**33** The black headed 'pin' moves successively from the vertical to the horizontal and returns to the vertical. Next time it should be vertical. The white headed 'pin' moves successively from the '13.30' position, the 12.00 position, the 10.30 position and then to the 09.00 position where it is hidden by the black headed pin. Next, it should be in the 07.30 position; answer 'a'.

**34** The outside square rotates. The inside square remains in the same position, whilst the small circle within it changes shade from white to black and moves down progressively from top right to bottom right.

**35** Only 'b' has one internal line, the others have two.

**36** The black circle moves from right to left of its line so that its next position will be right. The white circle moves at the head of its line successively from 15.00, to 12.00, to 09.00 and to 06.00 so that its next position will be at 03.00. Note that in the first drawing the white circle was covered or 'hidden' by the black circle, which will happen next time, so answer 'b'.

**37** Only in 'a' is there a single small white figure in the large square; there are two white figures inside all three of the other squares.

**38** In successive drawings a black circle moves from top left to bottom right of a circle, whilst a semi-circular 'plate' rotates anti-clockwise around the circle. In the third drawing the 'plate' has rotated to the left hand side of the circle and covers the black circle at top left. In the fourth drawing the 'plate' has rotated and covers the circle at bottom right. The black circle will next be at top left of the large circle, exposed by the 'plate', which has rotated to the right hand side; answer 'c'.

**39** Only in answer 'd' is there a circle juxtaposed to the side of each line.

# Test 2 Numerical Insight

This is a test of how well you are able to perceive numerical relationships. From the four alternatives provided you have to choose the one that goes with the others.

You can mark your answer on the page in the way that suits you best. You can cross the correct answer through, mark with a tick, circle or underline. It is best to mark your answer with a pencil so that you can erase it if you change your mind. The first of the examples below has been done already.

**Examples**

| 1 | 1 | 4 | 2 | 6 | 5 |
|---|---|---|---|---|---|
|   | 2 | 9 | 8 | 3 |   |
|   | a | b | c | d |   |

| 2 | 15 | 51 | 24 | 33 | 60 |
|---|----|----|----|----|----|
|   | 7  | 4  | 5  | 6  |    |
|   | a  | b  | c  | d  |    |

| 3 | 8 | 6 | 12 | 14 | 10 |
|---|---|---|----|----|----|
|   | 3 | 2 | 7  | 5  |    |
|   | a | b | c  | d  |    |

In the first example a '3' can be added to make a series from 1 to 6, so '3' has been underlined to show it is the correct answer. In the second example all the pairs of numbers total '6', so 'd' is the correct answer. In the third example the correct answer is '2' for several reasons: because it is an even number, like those above, and because it divides into the numbers above and because the numbers above ascend (or descend) by 2. In this example, none of the other numbers, 3, 7 or 5, will work as well.

This test lasts 15 minutes. You have to work accurately and do as many questions as you can in the time allowed. When you are ready, start the test that begins over the page and start your timer as you do so. Keep going until you have finished the last question or run out of time.

| **1** | **2** | **2** | **2** | **2** | **2** |
|---|---|---|---|---|---|
| | 3 | 4 | 2 | 5 | |
| | a | b | c | d | |

| **2** | **6** | **3** | **4** | **2** | **1** |
|---|---|---|---|---|---|
| | 5 | 4 | 0 | 8 | |
| | a | b | c | d | |

| **3** | **6** | **6** | **6** | **6** | **6** |
|---|---|---|---|---|---|
| | 7 | 3 | 8 | 10 | |
| | a | b | c | d | |

| **4** | **2** | **6** | **4** | **10** | **12** |
|---|---|---|---|---|---|
| | 8 | 16 | 14 | 1 | |
| | a | b | c | d | |

| **5** | **3** | **6** | **9** | **15** | **12** |
|---|---|---|---|---|---|
| | 2 | 21 | 24 | 18 | |
| | a | b | c | d | |

| **6** | **1** | **3** | **2** | **4** | **5** |
|---|---|---|---|---|---|
| | 16 | 15 | 9 | 7 | |
| | a | b | c | d | |

| **7** | **4** | **12** | **8** | **10** | **2** |
|---|---|---|---|---|---|
| | 3 | 13 | 5 | 2 | |
| | a | b | c | d | |

| **8** | **49** | **56** | **21** | **84** | **91** |
|---|---|---|---|---|---|
| | 7 | 8 | 11 | 13 | |
| | a | b | c | d | |

| **9** | **100** | **60** | **1020** | **70** | **110** |
|---|---|---|---|---|---|
| | 111 | 85 | 35 | 80 | |
| | a | b | c | d | |

| **10** | **36** | **60** | **72** | **48** | **84** |
|---|---|---|---|---|---|
| | 40 | 12 | 96 | 18 | |
| | a | b | c | d | |

| **11** | **15** | **5** | **10** | **25** | **30** |
|---|---|---|---|---|---|
| | 23 | 20 | 15 | 85 | |
| | a | b | c | d | |

| **12** | **4** | **120** | **12** | **68** | **88** |
|---|---|---|---|---|---|
| | 3 | 2 | 6 | 5 | |
| | a | b | c | d | |

| **13** | **39** | **48** | **27** | **51** | **57** |
|---|---|---|---|---|---|
| | 54 | 13 | 3 | 7 | |
| | a | b | c | d | |

| **14** | **91** | **56** | **35** | **140** | **63** |
|---|---|---|---|---|---|
| | 107 | 4 | 7 | 9 | |
| | a | b | c | d | |

| **15** | **8** | **64** | **2** | **4** | **32** |
|---|---|---|---|---|---|
| | 1 | 16 | 12 | 48 | |
| | a | b | c | d | |

| **16** | **735** | **591** | **663** | **366** | **87** |
|---|---|---|---|---|---|
| | 94 | 443 | 89 | 4443 | |
| | a | b | c | d | |

| **17** | **6** | **11** | **27** | **18** | **38** |
|---|---|---|---|---|---|
| | 4 | 9 | 2 | 5 | |
| | a | b | c | d | |

| **18** | **58** | **135** | **25** | **51** | **5** |
|---|---|---|---|---|---|
| | 35 | 46 | 111 | 39 | |
| | a | b | c | d | |

**19**  74      92      58      34      36
        31      52      48      79
        a       b       c       d

**20**  97      42      53      86      31
        2       4       28      5
        a       b       c       d

**21**  11      16      26      21      6
        14      3       5       33
        a       b       c       d

**22**  3549    4827    1758    4935    5817
        6077    7491    4819    994
        a       b       c       d

**23**  7642    9321    82      21      532
        431     3       1802    7660
        a       b       c       d

**24**  112     459     358     224     404
        164     336     183     247
        a       b       c       d

**25**  7765    979     555     96      898
        469     98      707     43242
        a       b       c       d

**26**  902     6010    7064    5093    110
        11      8994    202     2146
        a       b       c       d

**27**  7663    6877    4008    2113    55
        4202    969     42      330
        a       b       c       d

**28**   **4132**   **9678**   **8493**   **5894**   3461

    9788   5473   1490   7889

    a       b       c       d


**29**   **13**   **17**   **14**   **19**   10

    2       18      29      8

    a       b       c       d


**30**   **28**   **26**   **52**   **72**   29

    21      24      32      82

    a       b       c       d

# Answers to Test 2

| | | | | | | | | | |
|---|---|---|---|---|---|---|---|---|---|
| **1** | c | **7** | d | **13** | c | **19** | b | **25** | d |
| **2** | a | **8** | a | **14** | c | **20** | a | **26** | c |
| **3** | b | **9** | d | **15** | b | **21** | c | **27** | d |
| **4** | a | **10** | b | **16** | d | **22** | b | **28** | a |
| **5** | d | **11** | b | **17** | c | **23** | c | **29** | b |
| **6** | b | **12** | b | **18** | a | **24** | b | **30** | b |

RAW SCORE = Number of correct answers minus $^1/_5$ of incorrect answers.

GRADES

| | |
|---|---|
| A score of 20 or over | grade A |
| 16–19 | grade B |
| 11–15 | grade C |
| 7–10 | grade D |
| 4–6 | grade E |
| 0–3 | grade F |

Transfer your grade to the chart on page 94.

# Explanations to Test 2

## Numerical Insight

1    The answer is 'c' because it is the same number as the others in the line.
2    The answer is 'a' because the number 5 is missing from the sequence.
3    The answer is 'b' because it divides into 6. No other answer has a satisfactory connection.
4    The answer is 'a' because 8 is missing from the series.
5    '18' is missing in the series of ascending threes.
6    Adding the numbers produces answer 'b'.
7    All the numbers are divisible by 2.

**8**   All the numbers are divisible by 7.

**9**   Answer 'd' has a zero, like the others in the line.

**10**   All the numbers are divisible by 12. Why should the answer not be 96, answer 'c', which is next in sequence? It would have been a satisfactory answer had 12 not been offered; 12 is a better answer because it is the connective link between all the numbers. It is worth reminding oneself, especially on a timed test, to check all the possible answers provided and not to go for the one that may look obvious.

**11**   Answer 'b' is missing from the series.

**12**   All the numbers are divisible by 2.

**13**   All the numbers are divisible by 3.

**14**   All the numbers are divisible by 7.

**15**   Each number is doubled each time to form a sequence in which 16 is missing.

**16**   All of the numbers add to 15 as answer 'd'.

**17**   The difference between the ascending series increases by 2, thus 5, 7, 9, 11.

**18**   All these numbers contain a 5.

**19**   All the individual numbers add to odd numbers, thus 52; $5 + 2 = 7$.

**20**   All the individual numbers, when added, are divisible by 2.

**21**   '5' is the number by which the series ascends.

**22**   Adding the numbers together in each group produces 21.

**23**   All of the numbers has a 2.

**24**   The first two numbers add to the third number.

**25**   Each set of numbers when added is divisible by 5.

**26**   'C' is the only number to have a zero, like the line of numbers.

**27**   The first digit of each set makes an ascending series.

**28**   The first two numbers always adds to the second two numbers when added.

**29**   The number, 1, is a common digit to all items.

**30**   The difference between the two digits makes an ascending series, of which the answer, 'b', is 6.

# Test 3 Verbal Concepts

This is a test of how well you are able to perceive connections between words. You are given a question and some alternative words. From the alternatives provided you have to choose the one word that makes the most sense.

You can mark your answer on the page in the way that suits you best. You can cross the correct answer through, mark with a tick, circle or underline. It is best to mark your answer with a pencil so that you can erase it if you change your mind. The first of the examples below has been done already.

## Examples

**1**    Which word describes something different from the others?

| ROAD | HOUSE | RESIDENCE | HOME |
|------|-------|-----------|------|
| <u>a</u> | b | c | d |

**2**    Which word is closest in meaning to the word CONNECT?

| ATTACH | DULL | FETCH | SNAP |
|--------|------|-------|------|
| a | b | c | d |

In the first example 'ROAD' is the odd one out because the others are all to do with a place in which to live. In the second example 'CONNECT' is a verb meaning 'to join', as is 'ATTACH'. The other words mean something different: 'dull' is an adjective; 'fetch' is a verb, but means 'to bring'; 'SNAP' is a noun describing a quick, closing sound.

This test lasts 10 minutes. You have to work accurately and do as many questions as you can in the time allowed. When you are ready, start the test that begins over the page and start your timer as you do so. Keep going until you have finished the last question or run out of time.

**1** Which word describes something different from the others?

| BLUE | YELLOW | SHOES | GREEN |
|------|--------|-------|-------|
| a | b | c | d |

**2** Which word is closest in meaning to the word NOISE?

| ROAD | SOUND | MAN | QUIET |
|------|-------|-----|-------|
| a | b | c | d |

**3** Which word describes something different from the others?

| SKILFUL | TALENTED | CLEVER | INCAPABLE |
|---------|----------|--------|-----------|
| a | b | c | d |

**4** Which word is closest in meaning to the word STRANGE?

| FINE | ODD | NORMAL | RESPECT |
|------|-----|--------|---------|
| a | b | c | d |

**5** Which word describes something different from the others?

| BANG | HASTY | RAPID | QUICK |
|------|-------|-------|-------|
| a | b | c | d |

**6** Which word is closest in meaning to the word FIX?

| EXPAND | REPAIR | REMOVE | REVEAL |
|--------|--------|--------|--------|
| a | b | c | d |

**7** Which word describes something different from the others?

| CRATER | GULF | LUMP | PIT |
|--------|------|------|-----|
| a | b | c | d |

**8** Which word is closest in meaning to the word PATH?

| TRACK | OUTLET | LAND | HILL |
|-------|--------|------|------|
| a | b | c | d |

**9** Which word describes something different from the others?

| RECORD | REPORT | STATE | SPEAK |
|--------|--------|-------|-------|
| a | b | c | d |

**10** Which word is closest in meaning to the word COLLECT?

| FORFEIT | GATHER | PROPERTY | SHIFT |
|---------|--------|----------|-------|
| a | b | c | d |

**11** Which word describes something different from the others?

| FACTUAL | AUTHENTIC | IMAGINARY | REAL |
|---------|-----------|-----------|------|
| a | b | c | d |

**12**   Which word is closest in meaning to the word INCLUDE?

| CONTAIN | EXTRA | SUBTRACT | CONFORM |
|---------|-------|----------|---------|
| a | b | c | d |

**13**   Which word describes something different from the others?

| EXPERT | MASTER | ACE | BUNGLER |
|--------|--------|-----|---------|
| a | b | c | d |

**14**   Which word is closest in meaning to the word GUARDIAN?

| GRANTEE | LICENSEE | TRUSTEE | EMPLOYEE |
|---------|----------|---------|----------|
| a | b | c | d |

**15**   Which word describes something different from the others?

| INCESSANT | TRANSITORY | RELENTLESS | INTERMINABLE |
|-----------|------------|------------|--------------|
| a | b | c | d |

**16**   Which word is closest in meaning to the word DESIGN?

| MISCONCEIVE | SHOCK | APATHY | PURPOSE |
|-------------|-------|--------|---------|
| a | b | c | d |

**17**   Which word describes something different from the others?

| GAIN | INTEREST | HARM | PROFIT |
|------|----------|------|--------|
| a | b | c | d |

**18**   Which word is closest in meaning to the word FRANTIC?

| FRENETIC | SANE | FOOLISH | DISPOSSESSED |
|----------|------|---------|--------------|
| a | b | c | d |

**19**   Which word describes something different from the others?

| POSITION | DOCK | BED | FLOWER |
|----------|------|-----|--------|
| a | b | c | d |

**20**   Which word is closest in meaning to the word RESTORATION?

| CONTINUATION | RESTITUTION | RELAXATION | APPRECIATION |
|--------------|-------------|------------|--------------|
| a | b | c | d |

**21**   Which word describes something different from the others?

| ENQUIRY | BIOGRAPHY | HISTORY | MEMOIR |
|---------|-----------|---------|--------|
| a | b | c | d |

**22**   Which word is closest in meaning to the word HINDER?

| BACK | DIFFICULTY | OBLIGE | HAMPER |
|------|------------|--------|--------|
| a | b | c | d |

**23** Which word describes something different from the others?

| INVENTORY | RECORD | RECKON | CATALOGUE |
|---|---|---|---|
| a | b | c | d |

**24** Which word is closest in meaning to the word INSTANCE?

| EVENTUAL | ILLUSTRATION | ERROR | RESTRICTION |
|---|---|---|---|
| a | b | c | d |

**25** Which word describes something different from the others?

| RADIANCE | BLAST | OUTBURST | HARSH |
|---|---|---|---|
| a | b | c | d |

**26** Which word is closest in meaning to the word NONCHALANT?

| COAXING | ELOQUENT | COOL | ENTHUSIASTIC |
|---|---|---|---|
| a | b | c | d |

**27** Which word describes something different from the others?

| BARREN | DESOLATED | FORLORN | FLAWED |
|---|---|---|---|
| a | b | c | d |

**28** Which word is closest in meaning to the word CURT?

| VERBOSE | LONG | ABRUPT | FRANK |
|---|---|---|---|
| a | b | c | d |

**29** Which word describes something different from the others?

| TOKEN | SIGN | REMNANT | UNDEVELOPED |
|---|---|---|---|
| a | b | c | d |

**30** Which word is closest in meaning to the word SPHERE?

| PLACE | SPACIOUS | SHAPE | ORB |
|---|---|---|---|
| a | b | c | d |

**31** Which word describes something different from the others?

| NAB | NAIL | COLLAR | STICK |
|---|---|---|---|
| a | b | c | d |

**32** Which word is closest in meaning to the word CHARY?

| HEEDLESS | SHY | RUSH | PLANNED |
|---|---|---|---|
| a | b | c | d |

**33** Which word describes something different from the others?

| EXULT | EULOGIZE | SOLEMNIZE | ENTERPRISE |
|---|---|---|---|
| a | b | c | d |

**34**  Which word is closest in meaning to the word UNSTEADY?

| UNCHANGEABLE | SATURNINE | MERCURIAL | UNVARIED |
|---|---|---|---|
| a | b | c | d |

**35**  Which word describes something different from the others?

| MELD | SECEDE | MERGER | FUSE |
|---|---|---|---|
| a | b | c | d |

**36**  Which word is closest in meaning to the word GENIAL?

| CONVIVIAL | TWIN | ESCORT | RAPPORT |
|---|---|---|---|
| a | b | c | d |

**37**  Which word describes something different from the others?

| OPPRESSIVE | ONEROUS | INSOUCIANT | HERCULEAN |
|---|---|---|---|
| a | b | c | d |

**38**  Which word is closest in meaning to the word PREVARICATE?

| EQUIVOCATE | PREMEDITATE | RUMINATE | OFFICIATE |
|---|---|---|---|
| a | b | c | d |

**39**  Which word describes something different from the others?

| DOGGED | ASSIDUOUS | SEDULOUS | DILATORY |
|---|---|---|---|
| a | b | c | d |

**40**  Which word is closest in meaning to the word VAPID?

| SARDONIC | FUMY | STEAMY | VACUOUS |
|---|---|---|---|
| a | b | c | d |

# Answers to Test 3

| | | | | | | | | | |
|---|---|---|---|---|---|---|---|---|---|
| **1** | c | **9** | a | **17** | c | **25** | d | **33** | d |
| **2** | b | **10** | b | **18** | a | **26** | c | **34** | c |
| **3** | d | **11** | c | **19** | d | **27** | d | **35** | b |
| **4** | b | **12** | a | **20** | b | **28** | c | **36** | a |
| **5** | a | **13** | d | **21** | a | **29** | d | **37** | c |
| **6** | b | **14** | c | **22** | d | **30** | d | **38** | a |
| **7** | c | **15** | b | **23** | c | **31** | d | **39** | d |
| **8** | a | **16** | d | **24** | b | **32** | b | **40** | d |

RAW SCORE = Number of correct answers minus ¼ incorrect answers plus 4 if aged under 18 years, plus 2 if aged under 21 years.

GRADES

| | |
|---|---|
| A score of 35 or over | grade A |
| 29–34 | grade B |
| 23–28 | grade C |
| 17–22 | grade D |
| 10–16 | grade E |
| 0–9 | grade F |

Transfer your grade to the chart on page 94.

# Explanations to Test 3

## Verbal Concepts

1    All but 'c' are colours.
2    A 'noise' is a 'sound'. 'Quiet' is an opposite of 'noise', whilst 'road' and 'man' have no connection.
3    'Skilful', 'talented' and 'clever' are to do with competence, whilst 'incapable' means the opposite.
4    Both 'strange' and 'odd' mean something out of the ordinary or unusual.

**5**   A 'bang' is a loud, sudden, explosive sound and is a noun, whilst the other words are adjectives describing speediness.

**6**   'Fix' and 'repair' both mean to join together or to set right again.

**7**   A 'lump' is a protuberance, whilst the other words describe some form of cavity or indentation.

**8**   Both 'track' and 'path' describe a line of travel.

**9**   To 'record' is the only word among the four that describes a permanent act of setting down in a permanent form. A 'report' may also do this, but is not a necessary condition of reporting.

**10**  Both 'collect' and 'gather' describe bringing together or harnessing.

**11**  All but what is 'imaginary' can be objectively observed and authenticated.

**12**  Both 'include' and 'contain' describe the holding of contents or comprising.

**13**  All, apart from 'bungler' describe excellence of execution.

**14**  Both 'trustee' and 'guardian' mean to manage or look after the affairs of another.

**15**  All but 'transitory' describe a permanent, continuing action.

**16**  Both 'design' and 'purpose' describe the intent of carrying out an action.

**17**  All but 'harm' describe a beneficial increase.

**18**  Both 'frantic' and 'frenetic' describe wild excitement.

**19**  All but 'flower' describe a place, seat or situation occupied by a thing.

**20**  Both 'restoration' and 'restitution' mean to put back to the original state.

**21**  'Enquiry' means to question or to investigate, whereas the other words all describe a version of events.

**22**  Both 'hinder' and 'hamper' describe obstruction of movement.

**23**  'Reckon' is the act of ascertaining a number or amount, whilst the other words are all forms of a list for remembering.

**24**  Both 'instance' and 'illustration' are examples or representations of a thing.

**25** All but 'harsh' describe an emanation or emission from a centre.

**26** Both 'nonchalant' and 'cool' mean indifferent or unmoved.

**27** All but 'flawed' describe a bleak situation.

**28** The words 'curt' and 'abrupt' share brevity and suddenness, bordering upon discourtesy or being at odds with what has taken place thus far.

**29** 'A', 'b' and 'c' are all evidence of the existence of something else.

**30** Only 'sphere' and 'orb' share the concept of roundness.

**31** All but 'stick' share the concept of securing or getting hold of.

**32** Both 'chary' and 'shy' describe caution or wariness.

**33** All but 'd', which is a noun describing an undertaking, are verbs describing rejoicing or celebration.

**34** Both 'unsteady' and 'mercurial' describe quickness to change.

**35** 'Secede' describes withdrawing from, whilst the other words describe joining.

**36** Both 'genial' and 'convivial' describe cheerfulness and joviality.

**37** All but 'insouciant' describes difficult burdens.

**38** 'Prevaricate' and 'equivocate' share the concept of hesitation or uncertainty.

**39** 'Dilatory' describes delay, whilst the other words describe perseverance.

**40** Both 'vapid' and 'vacuous' share the concept of possessing nothing of interest or merit.

# Test 4 Form Recognition

This is a test of how well you are able to perceive differences between shapes. You have to choose the *one* shape that is EXACTLY the same as the original. The alternatives might be turned around as well as turned over. Try to imagine what the lines and shapes would look like from the other side. With each question you are only allowed to choose *one* of the alternatives as your answer.

You can mark your answer on the page in the way that suits you best. You can cross the correct answer through, mark with a tick, circle or underline. It is best to mark your answer with a pencil so that you can erase it if you change your mind. The first of the examples below has been done already.

**Examples**

In the first example only 'b' is exactly the same as the original. In the second example 'd' is exactly the same as the original seen from behind. In the other drawings, the shape is wrong or part of the drawing has been moved. In the third example 'a' is exactly the same as the original. In 'b' the small triangle is too large. In 'c' the shape is too large. In 'd' the shape is wrong.

This test lasts 9 minutes. You have to work accurately and do as many questions as you can in the time allowed. When you are ready, turn over the page and start your timer as you do so. Keep going until you have finished the last question or run out of time.

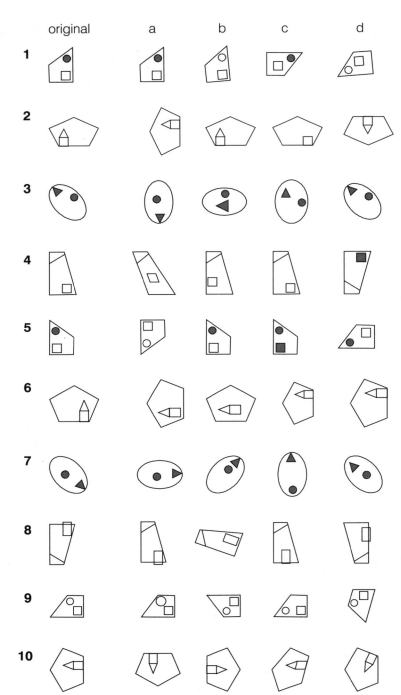

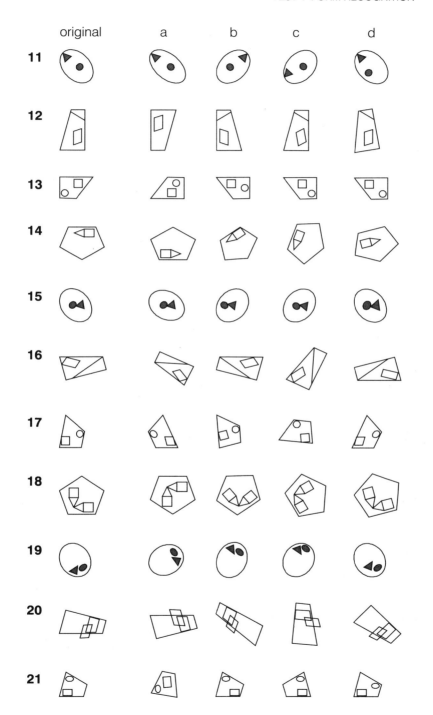

| original | a | b | c | d |
|----------|---|---|---|---|

**22**

**23**

**24**

**25**

**26**

**27**

**28**

**29**

**30**

**31**

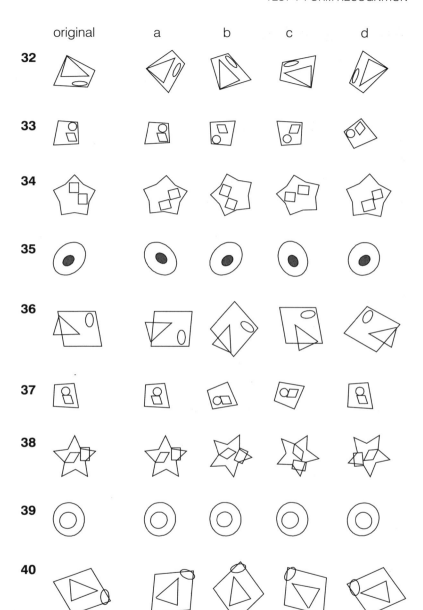

# Answers to Test 4

| 1 | a | 9 | b | 17 | c | 25 | d | 33 | d |
|---|---|---|---|----|---|----|---|----|---|
| 2 | b | 10 | a | 18 | c | 26 | c | 34 | a |
| 3 | d | 11 | b | 19 | a | 27 | a | 35 | c |
| 4 | c | 12 | b | 20 | d | 28 | b | 36 | d |
| 5 | b | 13 | d | 21 | c | 29 | a | 37 | c |
| 6 | d | 14 | a | 22 | b | 30 | b | 38 | d |
| 7 | a | 15 | c | 23 | d | 31 | b | 39 | d |
| 8 | a | 16 | c | 24 | a | 32 | c | 40 | b |

SCORE = Number of correct answers minus ¼ of incorrect answers.

GRADES

A score of  30 or over    grade A
            22–29         grade B
            15–21         grade C
            9–14          grade D
            4–8           grade E
            0–3           grade F

Transfer your grade to the chart on page 94.

# **Test 5** Extrapolation

This is a test of how well you are able to calculate an unknown term from a range of given terms.

Choose your answer FROM THE OPTIONS PROVIDED.

You can mark your answer on the page in the way that suits you best. You can cross the correct answer through, mark with a tick, circle or underline. It is best to mark your answer with a pencil so that you can erase it if you change your mind, but do not mark this book if it is not yours. Use spare paper instead. Also, have some spare paper available in case you need it for any rough work. The first of the examples below has been done already.

**Examples**

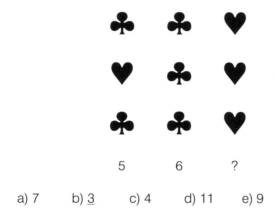

|   | 5 | 6 | ? |
|---|---|---|---|

a) 7      b) <u>3</u>      c) 4      d) 11      e) 9

In the first example, the value of a club must be '2', because in the second column three clubs totalled '6'. The value of a heart must be '1', because in the first column two clubs and a heart totalled '5'. It follows that a heart must be '1' less than a club. Therefore, the answer is 'b', 3.

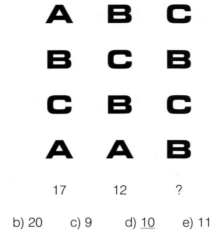

| A | B | C |
|---|---|---|
| B | C | B |
| C | B | C |
| A | A | B |
| 17 | 12 | ? |

a) 16    b) 20    c) 9    d) <u>10</u>    e) 11

In the second example, the second column is different from the first column as it has two B's instead of two A's. Therefore a B must be 5 less than an A. The only way that the second column can total '12' is for a B to value '1' and an A to have a value of '6'. This means that 'C' must value '4'. These values also give the correct total in the first column. No other values work. Introducing these values into the third column gives 10, so the answer is 'd', 10.

With each problem any term may have the same value as other terms. Remember to choose your answer from the options provided.

This test lasts 15 minutes. You have to work accurately and do as many questions as you can in the time allowed. Remember, you must choose an answer FROM THE OPTIONS PROVIDED. When you are ready, turn over the page and start your timer as you do so. Keep going until you have finished the last question or run out of time.

**1**

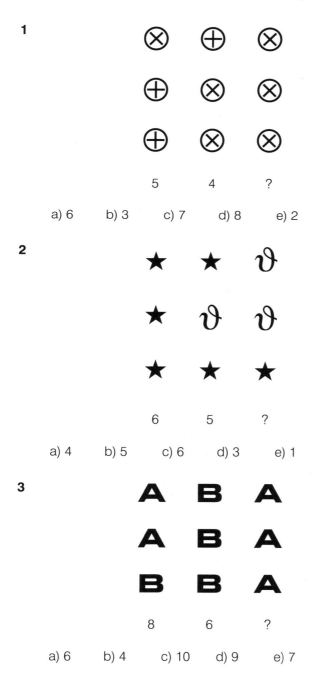

⊗   ⊕   ⊗

⊕   ⊗   ⊗

⊕   ⊗   ⊗

5    4    ?

a) 6    b) 3    c) 7    d) 8    e) 2

**2**

★   ★   ϑ

★   ϑ   ϑ

★   ★   ★

6    5    ?

a) 4    b) 5    c) 6    d) 3    e) 1

**3**

A   B   A

A   B   A

B   B   A

8    6    ?

a) 6    b) 4    c) 10    d) 9    e) 7

**4**

Ω   Ω   Ω

Ψ   Ω   Ψ

Ω   Ω   Ψ

5     3    ?

a) 4    b) 7    c) 6    d) 8    e) 2

**5**

h   v   h

v   h   h

v   h   h

8   13   ?

a) 15    b) 12    c) 17    d) 21    e) 18

**6**

Θ   Σ   Θ

Σ   Σ   Θ

Θ   Θ   Θ

8   10   ?

a) 6    b) 4    c) 10    d) 9    e) 7

**7**

$$\alpha \quad \gamma \quad \chi$$

$$\alpha \quad \gamma \quad \chi$$

$$\chi \quad \chi \quad \chi$$

5     5     ?

a) 6     b) 7     c) 9     d) 8     e) 10

**8**

$$2 \quad 7 \quad 2$$

$$2 \quad 7 \quad 7$$

$$2 \quad 7 \quad 2$$

9     12     ?

a) 18     b) 12     c) 15     d) 9     e) 10

**9**

11     13     ?

a) 15     b) 12     c) 9     d) 18     e) 21

**10**

| | | |
|---|---|---|
| A | B | B |
| A | A | B |
| C | C | C |
| A | A | C |
| 10 | 10 | ? |

a) 6    b) 7    c) 8    d) 9    e) 14

**11**

|  | | |
|---|---|---|
| 25 | 30 | ? |

a) 30    b) 20    c) 45    d) 35    e) 40

**12**

| | | |
|---|---|---|
| 9 | 11 | 12 |
| 9 | 11 | 12 |
| 11 | 12 | 11 |
| 11 | 9 | 11 |
| 14 | 12 | ? |

a) 8    b) 10    c) 6    d) 12    e) 9

**13**

9        12        ?

a) 11     b) 15     c) 12     d) 10     e) 13

**14**

17        28        ?

a) 42     b) 36     c) 48     d) 40     e) 56

**15**

| B | X | X | H |
|---|---|---|---|
| X | B | B | X |
| X | B | H | H |
| B | B | B | X |

14    13    16    ?

a) 17     b) 18     c) 19     d) 20     e) 21

**16**

| | | | |
|---|---|---|---|
| % | % | % | & |
| & | & | % | % |
| % | & | % | ! |
| & | & | ! | % |
| 34 | 29 | 41 | ? |

a) 36    b) 34    c) 42    d) 35    e) 28

**17**

| | | | |
|---|---|---|---|
| Y | Y | Ω | Y |
| Ω | Ω | Ξ | Ξ |
| Y | Ω | Ξ | Ω |
| Ξ | Ξ | Ω | Ξ |
| 50 | 45 | 32 | ? |

a) 30    b) 39    c) 41    d) 37    e) 35

# Answers to Test 5

| | | | | | | | |
|---|---|---|---|---|---|---|---|
| **1** | b | **6** | a | **10** | c | **14** | c |
| **2** | a | **7** | c | **11** | d | **15** | d |
| **3** | d | **8** | e | **12** | b | **16** | a |
| **4** | b | **9** | a | **13** | b | **17** | d |
| **5** | e | | | | | | |

RAW SCORE = Number of correct answers minus $\frac{1}{5}$ of incorrect answers.

GRADES

| A score of | 12 or over | grade A |
|---|---|---|
| | 9–11 | grade B |
| | 7–8 | grade C |
| | 5–6 | grade D |
| | 3–4 | grade E |
| | 1–2 | grade F |

Transfer your grade to the chart on page 94.

# Explanations to Test 5

## *Extrapolation*

**1**    In the first column the diagonal cross must have the value of either 1 or 3, since the straight crosses must have equal values and therefore be either 1 or 2. If the value of the diagonal cross is three then the second column would not be correct, since the two values of the diagonal crosses would have exceeded 4 even without adding the value of the straight cross. Applying the value of 1 to the diagonal crosses and two to the straight crosses produces the correct totals for all three columns.

**2**    In the first column three stars total six, so each star must have the value of 2. Two stars in the second column add to 4, which means that the $\vartheta$ shape must be 1. Two $\vartheta$ shapes and a star in the third column total 4.

**3**     As three B's in the second column total six each B must have the same value of 2. Deducting the value of the B (2) in the first column leaves two A's that must total 6. As each A must have a value of 3, the total for the third column is 9.

**4**     In column two there are three symbols that are the same, so the value of $\Omega$ is 1. Two of the same symbols in column one total two so, by substitution, the value of $\psi$ is three. Two threes and a one in the third column total 7.

Rather than attempting to compute these problems mentally, one way to solve them is by applying quadratic equations, as follows:

**5**

| | | | | | |
|---|---|---|---|---|---|
| 1st column | 1 h | + | 2 v | = 8 |
| 2nd column | 2 h | + | 1 v | = 13 |

Therefore (by multiplying the 2nd column by 2)

| | | | | | |
|---|---|---|---|---|---|
| 1st column | 1 h | + | 2 v | = 8 |
| 2nd column | 4 h | + | 2 v | = 26 |

Therefore (by subtracting the 1st from the 2nd column)

| | | |
|---|---|---|
| | 3 h | = 18 |
| Therefore | 1 h | = 6 |
| 3rd column | 3 h | = 18 |

**6**

| | | | | | |
|---|---|---|---|---|---|
| 1st column | 2 $\Theta$ | + | 1 $\Sigma$ | = 8 |
| 2nd column | 1 $\Theta$ | + | 2 $\Sigma$ | = 10 |

Therefore (by multiplying the 1st column by 2)

| | | | | | |
|---|---|---|---|---|---|
| 1st column | 4 $\Theta$ | + | 2 $\Sigma$ | = 16 |
| 2nd column | 1 $\Theta$ | + | 2 $\Sigma$ | = 10 |

Therefore (by subtracting the 2nd from the 1st column)

| | | |
|---|---|---|
| | 3 $\Theta$ | = 6 |
| Therefore | 1 $\Theta$ | = 2 |
| 3rd column | 3 $\Theta$ | = 6 |

**7**     Both the 1st and 2nd columns total 5. Therefore the values of $\alpha$ and $\gamma$ must be the same. If 2, then the value of $\chi$ will be 1, whereas, if 1, then the value of $\chi$ will be 3. Putting these values for $\chi$ into the third column would give totals of 9 or 3. Only 9 is provided as one of the possible answers.

**8**   The 2's have all the same value and equal nine so that a single 2 has the value of 3. The 7's all have the same value of 4. The answer is $3 + 4 + 3 = 10$.

**9**   Because there are 2 ↻ in column 1, which totals 11, and only 1 ↻ in column 2, which totals 13, it is obvious that the value of ⓪ is higher than that of ↻. Ascribing a value of 3 to ↻ and 5 to ⓪ gives correct totals for all three columns.

**10**   From the 1st and 2nd columns, which have the same total, the letter B must have the same value as the letter A. The possibilities are:

(i)   letters A and B are 1, which gives the letter C a value of 7
(ii)   letters A and B are 2, which gives the letter C a value of 4
(iii)   letters A and B are 3, which gives the letter C a value of 1

In the case of (i) the total for the 3rd column is $1 + 1 + 7 + 7 = 16$, in the case of (ii) the total is $2 + 2 + 4 + 4 = 12$, and in the case of (iii) the total is $3 + 3 + 1 + 1 = 8$, which is among the provided answers.

**11**   Column totals increase by 5 with each 🏛.

**12**   If the '9' has a value of 2 then the '11' has a value of 5 and value of '12' in the second column will be 0, so the 3rd column total will be 10. The same result can be obtained when the '9' has values of 3, 4, 5, 6 and 7.

**13**   Successively dropping ↻ with each column adds 3 to the total.

**14**   In the 2nd column ☞ has been replaced with a ?. The difference between the totals of the two columns show that ? has a value 11 more than ☞. If this value is put into the 2nd column then ☞ has a value of 0 and 🐇 has a value of 6. These values are then correct for the 1st column and the total for the 3rd column is therefore 44, although this is not provided among the answers. The value of ? can also be 12, giving ☞ a value of 1 and 🐇 a value of 3, so that this set of values gives the correct answer of 48.

**15**   Inspection of the 1st and 2nd columns shows that B has a value 1 less than X. A value of 4 for X and 3 for B gives the correct totals for the first two columns. Since the total for the third column is 16, the value for H must be 6 ($4 + 3 + H + 3 = 16$).

All the values have been found in order to arrive at the total for the 4th column.

**16**    Inspection of the 1st and 2nd columns shows that & has a value 5 less than %. A value of 6 is required for &, which gives % a value of 11. This would give ! a value of 8 in the third column. The fourth column is $6 + 11 + 8 + 11 = 36$.

**17**    The difference between the symbols between columns 2 and 3 show that $Y$ has a value of 13 more than $\Xi$. Between columns 1 and 2 a difference of value of 5 exists between $Y$ and $\Omega$. One strategy is to ascribe the lowest possible value, 0, to $\Xi$ in column 1. Because $Y$ is 13 more than this and 5 more than $\Omega$ it can be seen that 0 is too low a value for $\Xi$. Successive strategies could ascribe higher values for $\Xi$ until the sum fits the total, thus: $(1 + 14 + 9 + 14 = 38)$, $(4 + 17 + 12 + 17 = 50)$. When $Y$ is 17 and $\Xi$ is 4, the 4th column is $17 + 4 + 12 + 4 = 37$.

# Test 6 Technical

This is a test of how well you understand how machines work. You are given a picture or diagram and you have to answer the question. You must choose one of the answers provided.

You can mark your answer on the page in the way that suits you best. You can cross the correct answer through, mark with a tick, circle or underline. It is best to mark your answer with a pencil so that you can erase it if you change your mind. Have some spare paper available in case you need it for any rough work.

**Example**

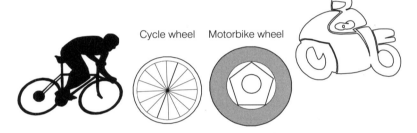

Cycle wheel    Motorbike wheel

As is shown in the diagram, motorbike wheels are larger than cycle wheels. If the cycle and the motorbike both travel for a kilometre, which type of wheel would have turned around the most times?

a) both the same    b) the cycle wheels    c) the motorbike wheels

The answer is B) because the distance around the motorbike wheel is longer than the cycle wheel, therefore the cycle wheel has to turn more times to travel the same distance.

In the test you have to look at each diagram and read the question carefully before making your answer. This test lasts 20 minutes. You have to work accurately and do as many questions as you can in the time allowed. The questions are not in order of difficulty.

When you are ready, turn over the page and start your timer as you do so. Keep going until you have finished the last question or run out of time.

**1**   Two wheels are touching so that one has to turn around if the other one turns. If wheel G is pushed anticlockwise in the direction shown by the arrow, which way will wheel K turn?

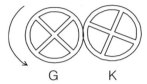

G        K

a) both the wheels remain stuck so that they do not move

b) clockwise

c) anticlockwise

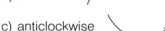

**2**   Three wheels are touching so that one has to turn around if the other one turns. If wheel M is pushed in the direction shown by the arrow, which way will wheel K turn?

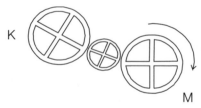

M

a) turns one way, then the other

b) anticlockwise

c) clockwise

d) becomes stuck

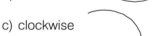

**3**   On a cycle the pedal wheel takes a chain to the gears on the back wheel. The chain passes around the middle gear. To make the cycle go faster, but to keep the pedal wheel turning at the same speed, which gear should the chain pass around?

Pedal wheel

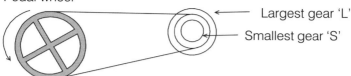

a) either

b) largest gear 'L'

c) smallest gear 'S'

**4**   Two cog wheels are touching so that one has to turn around if the other one turns. If wheel G is turned 4 times, how many times will wheel K turn?

a) both the wheels remain stuck so that they do not move

b) four times

c) three times

d) twice      e) once

G      K

**5**   Three wheels are touching, so that they all turn if any one turns. Which wheel turns the same way as R?

a) P

b) M

c) Neither P nor M

d) Both P and M

P

M

R

**6**   When P turns a quarter (¼) of a revolution in the direction shown, where does the handle, H, move to?

a) to the left and stop

b) left and right

c) right and left

d) right and stop

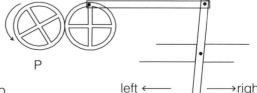

P

left ⟵      ⟶right

H

**7** At which point, P, S or T, would the boat be most safely attached with a rope to the bank?

a) P

b) S

c) T

d) all the same

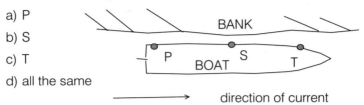

direction of current

**8** A snooker ball S is about to hit ball M so that M will collide with ball G. In which direction will ball G travel?

a)    b) ⟶

c)    d)

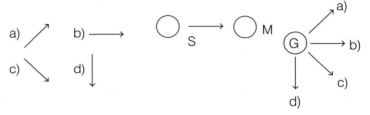

**9** The four drawings are of wooden gates between wooden posts. The gates are each fixed to a post on one side with hinges. Which gate is most likely to keep its shape if a child climbs on to it?

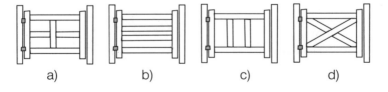

a)        b)        c)        d)

**10** A steel ball bearing hits a solid metal plate in the direction shown. In which direction will the ball continue after hitting the surface of the plate?

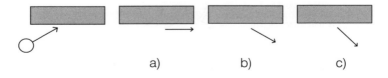

a)        b)        c)

**11** The water in a full swimming pool is clear. A man can see a ball that has sunk to the bottom. Where is the actual position of the ball likely to be?

a) P    b) S    c) T    d) R

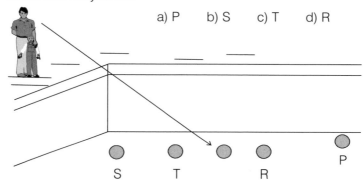

S          T          R                    P

**12** A band passes around wheels P and M. Another band passes around wheel R and the middle of wheel P. When R turns clockwise in the direction shown, which way does M turn?

a) clockwise

b) anticlockwise

c) M cannot turn

**13** All the wheels are touching, so that if one moves the others must also move. Which other wheel or wheels turn the same way as Z?

a) H              d) P and M

b) M              e) P and H

c) H and M    f) R and M

**14** At which point is the dam most likely to break?

a) at the top          d) in the middle

b) at the bottom     e) cannot tell

c) at the side

**15** If all the wheels are touching so that if one moves the others must also move, which wheel turns fastest?

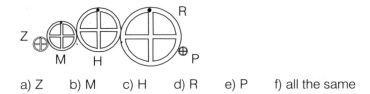

a) Z    b) M    c) H    d) R    e) P    f) all the same

**16** Whereabouts on the wheel is it fastest when it turns?

a) all the same    c) at J

b) at H    d) at G

**17** On a windless, clear day, a small motorboat wants to travel across a channel between two coasts from Port Z to Port W. In which direction should the boat be headed?

a) North

b) South

c) East

d) West

e) North East

f) North West

g) South East

h) South West

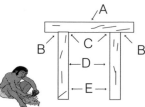

Direction of tide

**18** An ancient stone rests upon two others. At which point is it most likely to break?

a) at A    d) at D

b) at B    e) at E

c) at C

**19** When the thread rotates clockwise when looking from the right-hand side, which way does the cog wheel turn?

a) anticlockwise

b) clockwise

 right-hand side

**20** Which rudder position will turn a boat, moving dead ahead, towards the east?

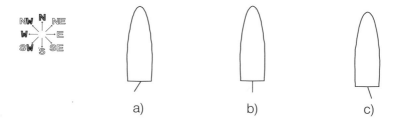

a)          b)          c)

**21** To get a spirit level to give a horizontal level, it needs to be pushed up at A, the right-hand side or, B, the left-hand side?

Left-hand side                          Right-hand side

a) right-hand side        b) left-hand side

**22** An old-fashioned grandfather clock can have its weight hung on either an iron bar or a strip of wood. Both pendulums look the same. Which one is more likely to lose time in hot weather, the one made of iron, R, or the one made of wood, W?

a) iron (R)

b) wood (W)

c) no difference

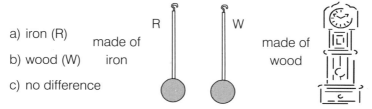

made of iron          made of wood

**23** In the diagrams, the letter T means the 'turning point', the letter P means the 'pressure' and the letter W means the 'weight'. Which of the diagrams describes the forces that are maintaining the climber in her position?

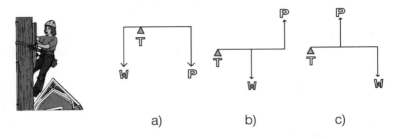

a)  b)  c)

**24** In relation to the earth and the sun, which position will the moon be in when there is a high tide on the earth at point H?

a)
b)
c)
d)

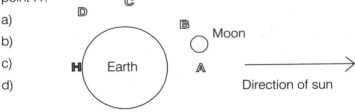

**25** To siphon liquid from the higher jar into the lower one, it would first be necessary to:

a) have a larger tube

b) have a longer tube

c) pour some of the liquid into the lower bottle to prevent air getting into the tube

d) push the top end of the tube further into the liquid

e) fill the tube with liquid

# Answers to Test 6

| | | | | | | | | | |
|---|---|---|---|---|---|---|---|---|---|
| **1** | b | **6** | a/b | **11** | c | **16** | d | **21** | b |
| **2** | c | **7** | a | **12** | b | **17** | h | **22** | a |
| **3** | c | **8** | c | **13** | f | **18** | a | **23** | c |
| **4** | d | **9** | d | **14** | e | **19** | a | **24** | a |
| **5** | c | **10** | b | **15** | e | **20** | c | **25** | e |

RAW SCORE = Number of correct answers minus $\frac{1}{3}$ of incorrect answers.

GRADES

| | |
|---|---|
| A score of 20 or over | grade A |
| 16–19 | grade B |
| 11–15 | grade C |
| 7–10 | grade D |
| 3–6 | grade E |
| 0–2 | grade F |

Transfer your grade to the chart on page 94.

# Explanations to Test 6

## *Technical*

1    Wheel G turns anticlockwise, which causes wheel K to rotate clockwise.
2    As wheel M turns clockwise, the small or middle wheel will turn anticlockwise, which causes wheel K to turn in the same way as M; that is, clockwise.
3    The smaller the gear, the shorter the 'distance' or the circumference around it. This 'distance' will be completed more quickly than the circumference or 'distance' of the middle or largest gear. The smallest or shortest 'distance' around the circumference will have the effect of causing the wheel to rotate more rapidly and therefore to travel the ground faster.

**4** Wheel G has 8 cogs whilst wheel K has 16, so K turns at half the speed or half the number of times as G.

**5** The effect of R is to turn the wheels it touches in an opposite rotation to itself.

**6** P causes the wheel it touches to rotate clockwise thus pushing the horizontal rod to the right, which causes the bottom part of the vertical rod to move to the left below the pivot at which point it stops, having completed a quarter turn. (Some particularly mechanically minded readers will surmise that it is critical to know the farthest distance between the pivot point at which the horizontal rod is attached to the wheel, and the farthest distance to the pivot at the end of the rod. This is because as the wheel rotates this maximum distance may be just before the wheel fully completes a quarter turn, this point being where the pivot on the wheel begins to descend and thus pulls the horizontal rod back to the left and therefore point H on the vertical rod to the right. From the drawing it looks as though this answer is the better one).

**7** At S and T the current will tend to pull the stern away from the bank with consequent strain to the rope as the anticlockwise moment increases.

**8** G will travel in a direction opposite to the side at which it is struck.

**9** Cross-braced timbers provide the support that is likely to stay most rigid. The weight is distributed through the diagonals and into the vertical supports. Gate D is therefore less likely to 'sag'.

**10** The ball hits the plate at an angle of about 30 degrees to the plate and will return from the plate at the same angle to the plate. Angle C is too great; the plate would have to have been concave for the ball to achieve this angle. Angle A is incorrect because it makes no allowance for the force in the ball that would return it from the solid metal plate with almost equal and opposite energy.

**11** Light bends as it travels from air into water, the angle bending away from the surface of the water, so that the ball appears nearer to the observer than it really is. Since the drawing does not contain all the necessary mathematics related to the angles, answer 'c' is an acceptable answer that shows understanding of the principle.

**12**   P has a band that passes around its middle, which has been crossed from R, and this has the same effect as if the two wheels were in direct contact, so that R travels in a clockwise direction and P anticlockwise. The band around P and M is not crossed and has the effect of making the wheels turn in the same direction.

**13**   As the wheels touch the direction of travel alternates from clockwise to anticlockwise. R and M are the two wheels that travel in opposite directions from Z.

**14**   Although pressure increases with the depth of water, the builders of the dam would have compensated by increasing the width or by using stronger materials. There is insufficient information to tell where the dam may be weakest.

**15**   P has the smaller circumference. Suppose R has 12 cogs, H 10 cogs, M 8 cogs, Z 6 cogs and P 4 cogs. If R moves 2 cogs it has turned by one sixth, H one fifth, M one quarter, Z one third and P by one half.

**16**   When the wheel turns, the greatest distance for the same amount of time is travelled at the circumference than at any other position on the radius.

**17**   The boat needs to head against the direction of the tide in order to counter its effect.

**18**   The stone is weakest in the middle where it has least support.

**19**   The effect of rotating the thread is to draw the cog towards the right and thus to turn the cog wheel anticlockwise.

**20**   The force of the rudder acts as a brake in which the rudder is turned so answer 'c' shows that the boat will 'brake' towards the east.

**21**   When the spirit level is horizontal the curved glass tube is marked at the highest point of its curve with a point of juncture with the air bubble, so the left-hand side needs to be raised.

**22**   Iron, though normally stronger than wood, is more susceptible to heat, expanding in hot weather. Expansion of the pendulum causes a slower beat of the pendulum so that the clock loses time.

**23**   The 'turning point' is the climber's feet, the 'weight' is her body and the 'pressure' is the strap that counteracts the weight, so that the 'pressure' is exerted between the 'turning point' and the 'weight'.

**24**   High tides form roughly at two places on the circumference of the earth in line with the position of the moon.

**25**   If the tube is first filled with liquid, the liquid will fall into the lower jar at the same time leaving a partial vacuum in the tube, the vacuum then drawing more liquid into the tube.

# Test 7 Analytical

This is a test of how well you are able to work out a sequence of information. You have to choose *two* numbers that will complete the sequence. All the possible answers are provided in the Chart.

Write *both* of your answers in the space at the end of each sequence. Both answers must be correct in order to obtain a score. It is best to mark your answer with a pencil so that you can erase it if you change your mind.

With each sequence of information try to find the outside shape first. Then find the inside shape. Then find whether the inside shape is blank, crossed or shaded. The first of the examples below has been done already.

## Chart

| | □ | ■ | ⊞ | ○ | ● | ⊕ | △ | ▲ | ⩕ |
|---|---|---|---|---|---|---|---|---|---|
| □ | 1 | 4 | 7 | 10 | 13 | 16 | 19 | 22 | 25 |
| ○ | 2 | 5 | 8 | 11 | 14 | 17 | 20 | 23 | 26 |
| △ | 3 | 6 | 9 | 12 | 15 | 18 | 21 | 24 | 27 |

(To use the chart, look along the three rows, which are large squares, circles or triangles, then look down the columns of small squares, circles or triangles. So, number 4 is a small, black square inside a large square, whilst number 15 is a small, black circle inside a large triangle, and so on.)

## Examples

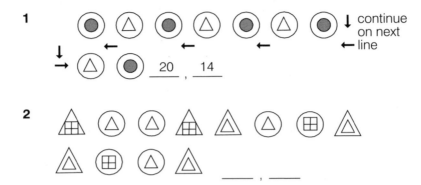

In the first example, the outside shape must be a circle because the sequence is 'circle, circle, circle', and so on, so you know the next two outside shapes are going to be a circle and then another circle. Then, the inside shape is 'circle, triangle, circle, triangle', and so on, so you know the next two inside shapes are going to be a triangle and then a circle. Then, the sequence in the small circles and triangles is 'black, white, black, white, black', and so on, so you know that the next figure must be white and the next figure must be black. Therefore, the answer is a large circle in which there is a white triangle, then a large circle in which there is a black circle. From the chart you get number 20 and then number 14. Both numbers are required to be correct.

In the second example the sequence of outside shapes is 'triangle, circle, circle, triangle, triangle, circle, circle, triangle' and so on, so the next two shapes must be a triangle then a circle. The inside shapes are 'square, triangle, triangle, square, triangle, triangle' and so on, so the next two inside shapes must be a square followed by a triangle. Then the shading inside the small figure is 'cross, white, white, cross, white, white', and so on, so the next two in the sequence must be a cross followed by white. The answer is '9, 20.'

It might help you to do a drawing so that you do not have to keep all the information in your head. Make sure you have spare paper available.

This test lasts 20 minutes. You have to work accurately and do as many questions as you can in the time allowed. When you are ready, turn over the page and start your timer as you do so. Keep going until you have finished the last question or run out of time.

## Chart

|  | □ | ■ | ⊞ | ○ | ● | ⊕ | △ | ▲ | ⊿ |
|---|---|---|---|---|---|---|---|---|---|
| □ | 1 | 4 | 7 | 10 | 13 | 16 | 19 | 22 | 25 |
| ○ | 2 | 5 | 8 | 11 | 14 | 17 | 20 | 23 | 26 |
| △ | 3 | 6 | 9 | 12 | 15 | 18 | 21 | 24 | 27 |

**1**

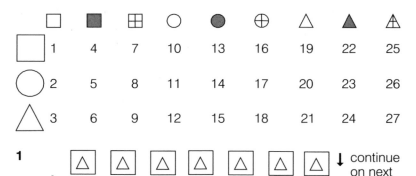

____ , ____

**2**

____ , ____

**3**

____ , ____

**4**

____ , ____

**5**

____ , ____

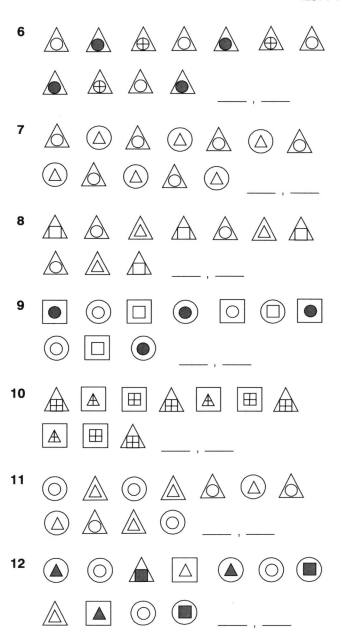

# Chart

**13**

**14**

**15**

**16**

**17**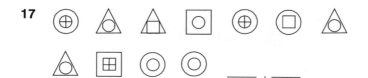

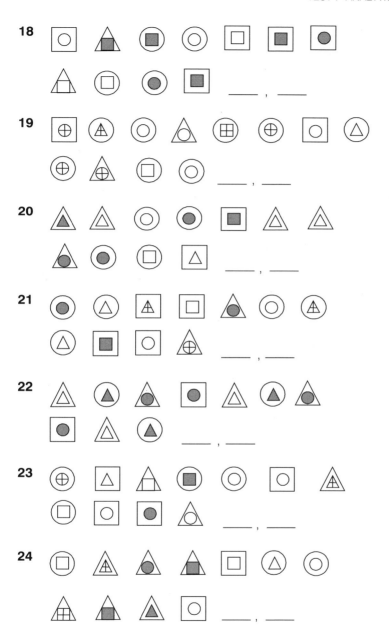

# *Chart*

**25**

**26**

**27**

# Answers to Test 7

| | | | | | |
|---|---|---|---|---|---|
| **1** | 19, 19 | **10** | 25, 7 | **19** | 16, 26 |
| **2** | 11, 20 | **11** | 21, 11 | **20** | 24, 15 |
| **3** | 21, 12 | **12** | 20, 24 | **21** | 20, 23 |
| **4** | 19, 19 | **13** | 11, 10 | **22** | 15, 13 |
| **5** | 11, 14 | **14** | 16, 14 | **23** | 20, 8 |
| **6** | 18, 12 | **15** | 2, 11 | **24** | 2, 2 |
| **7** | 12, 20 | **16** | 20, 13 | **25** | 20, 2 |
| **8** | 12, 21 | **17** | 3, 18 | **26** | 12, 19 |
| **9** | 10, 2 | **18** | 1, 10 | **27** | 15, 4 |

SCORE = Number of correct answers (both numbers correct).

GRADES

| A score of | 21 or over | grade A |
|---|---|---|
| | 17–20 | grade B |
| | 13–16 | grade C |
| | 9–12 | grade D |
| | 5–8 | grade E |
| | 0–4 | grade F |

Transfer your grade to the chart on page 94.

# Explanations to Test 7

## *Aptitudes*

**1**    The outside sequence is squares. The inner sequence is white triangles. The next two figures will be squares with white triangles inside.

**2**    The outside sequence is circles. The inside sequence is a white circle, white triangle, white circle, white triangle. The next outside figures will be a circle and another circle. The inside figures will be a white circle and a white triangle.

**3**    The outside sequence is triangles, so the next two figures will both be triangles. The sequence of inside figures is white circle, white triangle, white circle, white triangle, so the next two figures will have a white triangle and then a white circle.

4    The outside sequence is squares, so the next two figures will both be squares. The inside sequence is two white triangles and two white circles. The next two figures will both have a white triangle.

5    The outside sequence is circles so the next two will be plain circles. The inside has a sequence of four: black circle, black circle, white circle, white circle, so the next two will be: white circle, black circle.

6    The outside sequence is triangles, so the next two figures will both be triangles. The inside sequence is: white circle, black circle, crossed circle, so the next two figures will be: crossed circle, white circle.

7    The outside sequence is: triangle, circle, so the next two will be: triangle, circle. The inside sequence is: white circle, white triangle, so the next two will be circle, triangle.

8    The outside sequence is: triangle, triangle, so the next two will be triangles. The inside sequence is: white square, white circle, white triangle, so the next two will be: white circle, white triangle.

9    The outside sequence is: square, circle, so the next two figures will be: square, circle. The inside sequence is: circle, circle, square, so the next two will be: circle, square. The pattern sequence is: black, white, white, so the next two will be: white, white.

10   The outside sequence is: triangle, square, square, so the next two will be: square, square. The inside sequence is: triangle, square, square, so the next two will be: triangle, square. The pattern sequence is: crossed. Therefore: a crossed triangle in a large square and a crossed square in a large square.

11   The outside sequence is: circle, triangle, circle, triangle, triangle, so the next two will be: triangle, circle. The inside sequence is: circle, triangle, so the next two will be: triangle, circle. The pattern sequence is: white. Therefore: a white triangle in a large triangle and a white circle in a large circle.

12   The outside sequence is: circle, circle, circle, triangle, square, so the next two will be: circle, triangle. The inside sequence is: triangle, triangle, circle, square, so, the next two will be:

triangle, triangle. The pattern is: black, white, so the next two will be: white, black. So the next figure will be a white triangle in a large circle followed by a black triangle in a large triangle.

**13**   The outside sequence is: triangle, triangle, circle, square, square, so the next two will be: circle, square. The inside sequence is: circle, circle, circle, triangle, triangle, so the next two will be: circle, circle. The pattern is: white, white, cross, cross, cross, so the next two will be: white, white. So the next figure will be a white circle in a large circle followed by a white circle in a large square.

**14**   The outside sequence is: circle, triangle, square, so the next two will be: square, circle. The inside sequence is: circle, so the next two will be: circle, circle. The pattern is: black, black, white, cross, so the next two will be: cross, black. So the next figure will be a crossed triangle in a large square followed by a black triangle in a large circle.

**15**   The outside sequence is: triangle, circle, circle, so the next two will be: circle, circle. The inside sequence is: circle, circle, circle, square, square, square, so the next two will be: square, circle. The pattern is: white, white, cross, so the next two will be: white, white. So the next figure will be a white square in a large circle followed by a white circle in a large circle.

**16**   The outside sequence is: circle, circle, square, triangle, so the next two will be: circle, square. The inside sequence is: triangle, one circle, square, triangle, two circles, square, triangle, three circles, square, triangle, four circles, square, so the next two will be: triangle, circle. The pattern is: two white, three black, so the next two will be: white, black. So the next figure will be a white triangle in a large circle followed by a black circle in a large square.

**17**   The outside sequence is: 2 circles, 2 triangles, square, so the next two will be: triangle, triangle. The inside sequence is: 2 circles, square so the next two will be: square, circle. The pattern is: 3 white, cross, so the next two will be: white, cross. So the next figure will be a white square in a large triangle followed by a crossed circle in a large triangle.

**18**   The outside sequence is: 3 squares, triangle, 2 circles, so the next two will be: square, square. The inside sequence is: circle, 2 squares, so the next two will be: square, circle. The pattern is: 2 black, 2 white, so the next two will be: white, white. So the next figure will be a white square in a large square followed by a white circle in a large square.

**19**   The outside sequence is: 2 circles, triangle, 2 circles, square, so the next two will be: square, circle. The inside sequence is: square, 2 circles, triangle, 2 circles, so the next two will be: circle, triangle. The pattern is: 2 white, 2 crossed, so the next two will be: cross, cross. So the next figure will be a crossed circle in a large square followed by a crossed triangle in a large circle.

**20**   The outside sequence is: triangle, triangle, circle, circle, square, so the next two will be: triangle, triangle. The inside sequence is: 2 triangles, 2 circles, square, so the next two will be: triangle, circle. The pattern is: 2 black, 2 white, so the next two will be: black, black. So the next figure will be a black triangle in a large triangle followed by a black circle in a large triangle.

**21**   The outside sequence is: 3 circles, 2 squares, triangle, so the next two will be: circle, circle. The inside sequence is: 2 circles, 2 triangles, square, so the next two will be: triangle, triangle. The pattern is: white, black, white, cross, so: white, black. So the next figure will be a white triangle in a large circle followed by a black triangle in a large circle.

**22**   The outside sequence is:  triangle, circle, triangle, square, so the next two will be: triangle, square. The inside sequence is: 2 triangles, 2 circles, so the next two will be: circle, circle. The pattern is: 3 black, white, so the next two will be: black, black. So the next figure will be a black circle in a large triangle followed by a black circle in a large square.

**23**   The outside sequence is: square, triangle, 2 circles, square, triangle, 1 circle, then 2 squares (so the triangle only appears once in each sequence, whilst the squares and circles alternate between appearing once or twice), so the next two will be: circle, circle. The inside sequence is: circle, triangle, 2 squares, then 2 circles, triangle, square, then 3 circles (so the circles are increasing by 1 each sequence, whilst the triangles remain constant and the square always follow the triangle although it is not necessary to know how many squares will be in the next sequence since it is only necessary to deduce that there must be at least one), so the next two will be: triangle, square. The pattern is: 2 white, black, 2 whites, cross, so the next two will be: white, cross. So the next figure will be a white triangle in a large circle followed by a crossed square in a large circle.

**24**  The outside sequence is: 2 circle, 3 triangles, square, so the next two will be: circle, circle. The inside sequence is: 2 squares, triangle, circle, so the next two will be: square, square. The pattern is: 3 white, cross, 2 black, so the next two will be: white, white. So the next figure will be a white square in a large circle followed by a white square in a large circle.

**25**  The outside sequence is: 3 circles, triangle, square, so the next two will be: circle, circle. The inside sequence is: triangle, square, circle, triangle, 2 squares, so the next two will be: triangle, square. The pattern is: 2 white, black, 2 white, cross, so the next two will be: white, white. So the next figure will be a white triangle in a large circle followed by a white square in a large circle.

**26**  The outside sequence is: 2 triangles, 2 squares, circle, square, so the next two will be: triangle, square. The inside sequence is: 2 circles, triangle, 2 circles, square, so the next two will be: circle, triangle. The pattern is: white, cross, 2 white, black, 3 white, cross, (the number of whites increase by one, whilst the crosses and blacks alternate), so: white, white. So the next figure will be a white circle in a large triangle followed by a white triangle in a large square.

**27**  The outside sequence is: 2 triangles, square, circle, triangle, square, so the next two will be: triangle, square. The inside sequence is: square, circle, square, triangle, so the next two will be: circle, square. The pattern is: white, 2 blacks, cross, so the next two will be: black, black. So the next figure will be a black circle in a large triangle followed by a black square in a large square.

# How to Interpret and Apply Your Aptitudes

It is recommended that you complete as many of the aptitude tests as possible in order to profit from this chapter. Whilst even a single test result may be revealing, most insight will be gained if you are able to compare your strengths and weaknesses between different aptitudes.

Enter your results from the aptitude tests in the chart shown on page 94. You will need to put in an approximate position if your own score is between those printed in the chart. Then connect each of your results with a line. This will enable you to make an easy comparison between your effectiveness in different areas. Your completed chart will look something like that on page 93.

Your own profile is likely to be different and certainly different from that of anybody else's; there will be uniqueness about you that you can make use of. The differences between yourself and other people become even greater when you come to take your personality and interests into account! You can do this in later chapters.

It is up to you to decide how much meaning to place upon each one of your results and upon all of your results as a whole. So you will need to use your own judgement when it comes to finally grading yourself on each of the tests and also when it comes to interpreting the picture you are given. Thinking about how different you might be from the group upon which the grades have been based may lead you to make an adjustment to one or more of the grades you have obtained. Are you at an advantage or a disadvantage compared with the group?

There are many reasons why any one of your scores might need to be interpreted with latitude. These matters have been explained in the Introduction and it may be worthwhile to read that section again. Remember that the tests are intended to give you a guide; they are not intended to have, and nor could they have, the validity of tests that are administered by a professional psychologist, who would use fully researched tests and refer to statistical tables in order to make due allowance for your age, circumstances, health, education, and so on.

|  | F– F+ | E– E+ | D– D+ | C– C+ | B– B+ | A– A+ |
|---|---|---|---|---|---|---|
| Visual Logic | 5  9 | 10  14 | 15  19 | 20  25 | 26  31 | 32  39 |
| Numerical Insight | 1  3 | 4  6 | 7  10 | 11  15 | 16  19 | 20  22+ |
| Verbal Concepts | 5  9 | 10  14 | 17  22 | 23  28 | 29  34 | 35  40 |
| Form Recognition | 2  3 | 4  8 | 9  14 | 15  21 | 22  29 | 30  36 |
| Extrapolation | 1  2 | 3  4 | 5  6 | 7  8 | 9  11 | 12  14 |
| Technical | 1  2 | 3  6 | 7  10 | 11  15 | 16  19 | 20  23 |
| Analytical | 1  4 | 5  8 | 9  12 | 13  16 | 17  20 | 21  24 |

F– F+    E– E+    D– D+    C– C+    B– B+    A– A+

Bearing these points in mind, how does your profile match your attainments and experience? Does it reflect the results and qualifications you have already obtained? Are the strengths and weaknesses as you expected? Tests are only reliable to the extent that they have been designed properly and also administered correctly. As regards the latter, it is difficult to administer tests to yourself. In particular, errors in timing of even a second or two may affect your scores and timing yourself probably resulted in your spending a disproportionate amount of time watching the clock. Your test score may also vary slightly if you are feeling tired or unready. Again, this type of test does tend to penalize the slow but accurate worker who checks answers as he or she progresses. A psychologist would be looking carefully not just for your test score but also for signs of the manner in which you approached and tackled the test as this can be of as much importance. For these and other reasons, which are normally taken account of by someone who is professionally trained in testing, you may not have done as well on this occasion as you might do on another.

## Level of results

When you look at the overall level of the results you should be able to make some comparison with your own expectations in view of your history of performance in other tests and examinations.

| | F– | F+ | E– | E+ | D– | D+ | C– | C+ | B– | B+ | A– | A+ |
|---|---|---|---|---|---|---|---|---|---|---|---|---|
| Visual Logic | 5 | 9 | 10 | 14 | 15 | 19 | 20 | 25 | 26 | 31 | 32 | 39 |
| Numerical Insight | 1 | 3 | 4 | 6 | 7 | 10 | 11 | 15 | 16 | 19 | 20 | 22+ |
| Verbal Concepts | 5 | 9 | 10 | 14 | 17 | 22 | 23 | 28 | 29 | 34 | 35 | 40 |
| Form Recognition | 2 | 3 | 4 | 8 | 9 | 14 | 15 | 21 | 22 | 29 | 30 | 36 |
| Extrapolation | 1 | 2 | 3 | 4 | 5 | 6 | 7 | 8 | 9 | 11 | 12 | 14 |
| Technical | 1 | 2 | 3 | 6 | 7 | 10 | 11 | 15 | 16 | 19 | 20 | 23 |
| Analytical | 1 | 4 | 5 | 8 | 9 | 12 | 13 | 16 | 17 | 20 | 21 | 24 |

F– F+   E– E+   D– D+   C– C+   B– B+   A– A+

If your results are generally below average, you probably find timed examinations difficult or frustrating. Your intelligence may well emerge in ways that are not measured within the scope of this book; for example, you may find that expressive or practical subjects suit you better. If your results are generally above average, you are of a type who is able to apply themselves to the more conventional, academic courses that are usually assessed by means of timed examinations.

The level of your results gives you an indication of the ease with which you can tackle problems in certain areas. A very determined and conscientious individual can sometimes achieve more than the results suggest. Similarly, a less well-disciplined individual may underachieve generally. Nevertheless, the level of your results on these tests should be roughly in line with your experience. However, this book may have happily helped you to discover potential that you were not fully aware of beforehand.

## Pattern of results

There are two broad types of test and you should bear in mind what distinguishes them. If you have done better on the Verbal Concepts, Numerical Insight, Visual Logic and Analytical tests, you are likely to enjoy an academic route. If, on the other hand, you did better on the Technical and Form Recognition tests, you are more likely to enjoy areas that involve a more practical route into your profession. For many people, however, there is no clear distinction between these two broad groups and you will need to look further at the interpretations.

There are many possible results, but we will concentrate on the seven individual strengths, each of which is testing core, 'natural' potential, and then the 21 paired combinations that might emerge from two almost equally strong results. Look at your strongest score(s) to find out which profile is most representative of your underlying abilities.

Table of strongest aptitudes

|  | 2. Num. | 3. Verb. | 4. Form | 5. Extrap. | 6. Tech. | 7. Analyt. |
|---|---|---|---|---|---|---|
| 1. Visual logic | 8. | 9. | 10. | 11. | 12. | 13. |
| 2. Numerical insight |  | 14. | 15. | 16. | 17. | 18. |
| 3. Verbal concepts |  |  | 19. | 20. | 21. | 22. |
| 4. Form recognition |  |  |  | 23. | 24. | 25. |
| 5. Extrapolation |  |  |  |  | 26. | 27. |
| 6. Technical |  |  |  |  |  | 28. |

# *High scores on a single test*

## 1. Visual Logic

This test requires you to 'see' connections between concepts that are not described by either words or numbers. It is an abstract test that is less dependent upon learning than most of the other tests, so is often thought to reveal an aspect of natural 'raw' intelligence. It is frequently a good guide to potential for many scientifically based careers, but also to many others where acquiring and making sense of information is the essential requirement.

## 2. Numerical Insight

This aptitude is similar to, but not the same as, mathematical aptitude, because mathematics often requires other types of reasoning as well, for example on the visual or technical sides. The test requires an aptitude to 'think' with numbers and therefore is an essential requirement for many careers where practical as well as abstract calculations are made, including those related to economics and to science.

## 3. Verbal Concepts

This shows ability to reason with words and relates more to the written word, being the single most useful strength in any kind of formal, academic study within that branch termed the 'humanities'. This aptitude is often connected with literary and administrative careers, but is also a very important attribute in careers where writing is a major part, because it requires the ability to express yourself using the right word at the right time.

## 4. Form Recognition

This is the aptitude enabling you to visualize a three-dimensional object when given limited two-dimensional information. It can reveal the potential to 'read' drawings and understand physical layout that may be represented in other forms. The 'spatial' element is often seen in people who have an artistic or design understanding or skill.

## 5. Extrapolation

This is an abstract test of intelligence, considered by many psychologists to be one of the 'purest' measures of reasoning. It demands that you derive possibilities based upon available evidence, then form a hypothesis to test the problem. It is the kind of reasoning that often forms the essence of complex decision making where the outcome of a decision has to be assessed on the basis of implicit as opposed to objective data. Talent in this area suggests careers at senior levels in complex organizations involving law, finance and senior executive positions in business and public administration.

## 6.  Technical

This test reveals your understanding of the forces and dynamics that happen within and around machinery as well as in the natural world. Although the test items themselves are somewhat sophisticated, requiring a good understanding of language as well, this aptitude reveals a talent for many professions that have a connection with engineering, technology and 'hardware'.

## 7.  Analytical

This reveals potential for working out connections from a sequence of evidence where the key to the problem is embedded. Grasping the links between a series of events shows ability to think quickly, solve problems and to work with new ideas. Analytical reasoning does not always express itself in academic attainment, but nonetheless points to high-level, long-term potential.

# *High scores on two tests*

It is quite unusual to have one single strong ability and most people will want to see how two or more strengths might be applied.

## 8.  Visual/Numerical

These strengths are particularly for the harder-scientific approaches, especially at the senior levels. Examples in this area would include analytical chemists, metallurgists, astronomers, and nuclear physicists.

## 9.  Visual/Verbal

Some form of scientific or information or deductive career often suits this combination. People tend to be good in areas of the 'social' or 'biological' sciences.

## 10.  Visual/Form

This combines a logical approach with the ability to visualize. It reveals a good artistic sense as well as scientific potential. A career should ideally combine intuitive and deductive and rational elements in some way.

## 11.  Visual/Extrapolation

Activities combining these two strengths are often specialist, requiring a scientific or, in any case, logical approach and attention to order and detail. Programming and other information processing roles are possible in many different types of organization where data handing, record keeping and communication are important.

## 12.  Visual/Technical

This combines a scientific approach with the application of technical understanding. Technological careers are the obvious route, the precise areas perhaps being determined by neither factor, but rather how strong others factors might be. For example, the above with verbal aptitude might lead into administration and management, whilst numerical aptitude might suggest a more academic or research role.

## 13.  Visual/Analytical

This would include scientific and investigative areas of endeavour where the emphasis is upon reasoning, and understanding of knowledge, though not necessarily how to apply that knowledge.

## 14.  Numerical/Verbal

The ability to reason equally with words and numbers is often regarded as the best predictor of success in most formal, academic examinations that are not specifically scientific. There are numerous legal, administrative and financial careers that arise.

## 15.  Numerical/Form

This combination links the ability to use the design or sculptural aptitude with numbers. It also describes the potential of people who have been successful with computer software, web design and related areas.

## 16.   Numerical/Extrapolation

This combination is clearly most valuable in many areas of finance. Insurance, banking, actuarial work, statistics and many other areas connected with finance and administration are most obviously appropriate.

## 17.   Numerical/Technical

This is a common combination of applied science and technical fields as diverse as engineering, physics, geology, and production.

## 18.   Numerical/Analytical

These aptitudes suggest mathematical and therefore scientific areas of work where research and possibly innovation and deductive reasoning are required.

## 19.   Verbal/Form

This combination requires a means of expressing both the ability to use words and to work with design in some form. It could be applied in areas of, for example, photojournalism, magazine and film editing, directing, design consultancy and publishing.

## 20.   Verbal/Extrapolation

This is the area where you are dealing with words and having to do so with precision. Many 'office type' tasks fall into this category, particularly those that are legal. Connected with publishing, processing, translating, proofreading, personnel and many other areas of executive work.

## 21.   Verbal/Technical

This combination could lead into areas of work on the applied side of engineering dealing with legal issues, technical writing, lecturing and teaching, technical sales and other agents.

## 22.   Verbal/Analytical

This combination is frequently seen in people who are managers, directors, investigators or those who may have some kind of inter-pretative or consultancy responsibility. It is a combination that seems to lend itself to careers in which the management of others is a requirement.

## 23.   Form/Extrapolation

In this combination the artistic and design sense together with exactitude would have application in film editing and related areas of production, cartography, animation as well as more obviously technical areas such as electronics and programming.

## 24.   Form/Technical

This combination reveals extremely practical talent that might be expressed in many areas of industrial design, engineering and craft. A consideration would also be the hand–eye coordination, dexterity and other physical talents of the person.

## 25.   Form/Analytical

This combines the design sense, which is itself 'analytical', with a deductive approach, thus showing definite potential for 'seeing and sorting out'. This could take place in many practical areas of endeavour and may well include not only a project, but also the management of people.

## 26.   Extrapolation/Technical

This combination suggests functional, executive and technical careers in which dealing with material, equipment, budgets and resources would in some way be important.

## 27.   Technical/Analytical

This is relevant to process engineering, materials science and qual-ity control. It combines the ability to understand what happens with the abstract logic of why it happens. It often suggests managerial potential in a manufacturing or other active or physical context.

## 28.  Organizational/Extrapolation

This combination indicates ability to analyse and to think logically with attention to detail as well, and provides strong concentrative power and focus upon a task. This combination shows a penetrating mind that will be most effective when it can resolve problems and obtain an exact conclusion.

## *High scores on three or more tests*

There are, of course, other combinations of three or more strengths. Areas of weakness also need to be taken into account, as these show what it is probably best to avoid. You need to weigh up your own pattern, asking yourself 'Where would I be able to use this. . . , but would not be expected to have this. . . ?' The Occupational Index on page 161 should help you further with this process, and will also assist you in taking your personality and interests into account.

If you have abilities at a fairly even level, it is most important that you pay particular attention to your personality and to what will motivate you.

# PART TWO

# Personality

# Introduction

Testing personal and interpersonal skills has become increasingly popular in recent years. Organizations have become increasingly aware that the success of any enterprise is dependent to greater or lesser degree upon the manner in which you apply yourself to work and the way in which you relate to people. This is relevant to everyone at work where there is emphasis given to 'teamwork' and it is increasingly something that everyone is expected to take responsibility for, not just managers. This is explored fully in my book *Total Leadership*, also published by Kogan Page (see Bibliography).

Many tests of personality are now used for selection, development and awareness training. The more senior the position someone is applying for, the more critical a person's personality is likely to be. Such tests frequently contain deliberately ambiguous questions or apparently contradictory statements, because personality itself is elusive and difficult to measure. As you complete such questionnaires it is best not to be concerned about what the question is trying to get at. If you do this you might give quite the wrong impression, presenting a picture that is not you at all! Many questionnaires have a means by which the results can indicate whether a person has either been deliberately lying or unconsciously presenting a favourable impression. The best thing to do is to respond in the way that feels natural and correct for you. Any falsity in the description that emerges will then be due to either a) measurement error in the test or b) lack of awareness within you.

Personality tests are typically in the form that you will find in this book. Some tests, such as the Eysenck Personality Inventory, published by N.F.E.R., provide two comprehensive dimensions of personality, introversion and extroversion. Although it has only two dimensions, it is well regarded by scientists who have used it extensively for scientific research. Others, such as the Sixteen Personality Factor Questionnaire by Cattell, published by I.P.A.T., USA, and the Occupational Personality Questionnaire, published by Saville & Holdsworth Ltd, provide sixteen dimensions, although these are really just elaborations based upon four dimensions of assertiveness, independence, anxiety and sensitivity. Again, the Myers–Briggs Questionnaire, published by Consulting Psychologists Press, USA, has four dimensions of sensing, feeling, intuition and thinking. One of my own psychometric tests, the K6, published by Psychometrictests. com, has six dimensions of assertiveness, independence, factual, focus, creativity and emotionality. Generally, the same sorts of personality types or behaviours are 'wrapped up' by questionnaires in different ways. Recently, there has been much research suggesting that five factors of personality provide the most convenient ways to analyse a person, at least from the occupational testing point of view. For this reason I have provided a five-factor test within this volume as I hope that this will provide you with a convenient and modern way to think about your feelings and behaviour, and how these might relate to your career, the people you may meet in your career and the implications for your successful career progression.

# Five Factor Personality Test (CODIT)

This is a test of the way you do things and how you behave with people. You are given a sentence and you have to choose the statement that describes the way you usually behave or feel. You must choose one of the statements even though on some occasions the other statement could possibly also be true. Therefore, choose the statement that is true for you most of the time.

Of the two alternative statements you are given, both are equally 'good' or 'correct'. Neither is 'bad' or 'wrong'. They are about different ways that different people may behave and feel. You have to choose the statement that most describes you. Even though the statements might not describe you exactly all of the time, make a choice that is generally most true for you. Please place a tick in the box next to the statement that describes you. It is best to mark your answer with a pencil so that you can erase it if you change your mind.

We will call your completion of the questionnaire on yourself method a).

Alternatively, you can ask another person or persons to complete the questionnaire for the way they perceive you, which we will call method b). This method has several advantages. It will undoubtedly add to your own awareness of how other people perceive you since it is unlikely they will perceive you in the same way as you do yourself, not in all respects, anyway! It will considerably aid you when it comes to interpreting your scores, especially where your scores are borderline on some of the dimensions of personality, which is described in the next section. When you apply the questionnaire using method b) simply replace the word 'I' with the word 'you' in all of the statements below.

This test is not timed. However, it is best not to spend too long thinking about each item. Answer naturally in the way that is true for you. Start when you are ready.

**1**    When faced with unexpected events I:
   ☐ a)  know I can rise to the challenge
   ☐ b)  wonder if I can cope

**2**    I would rather my work:
   ☐ a)  brought me into constant contact with lots of people
   ☐ b)  allowed me to work by myself

**3**    In keeping an appointment I am more likely to arrive:
   ☐ a)  slightly early
   ☐ b)  slightly late

**4**    What I do is usually:
   ☐ a)  a good idea at the time
   ☐ b)  sensible

**5**    When working with people it is better when:
   ☐ a)  a single person says what to do
   ☐ b)  everybody discusses what to do

**6**    When I speak to people on almost any subject:
   ☐ a)  I believe that what I say is important
   ☐ b)  I think that what I say will probably be ignored

**7**    In a room full of strangers I would:
   ☐ a)  introduce myself to people
   ☐ b)  wait and see what people want to do

**8**    When I am attending to something important:
   ☐ a)  I do not like to be distracted by anything else
   ☐ b)  I like to attend to other things as well

**9**    I would be more interested in:
   ☐ a)  a poem about being a child
   ☐ b)  an article about the history of the conquest of space

**10**   People who work together are happiest when:
   ☐ a)  they know what their own task is
   ☐ b)  they are aware how they feel about each other

**11**   People feel that if asked to do something difficult:
   ☐ a)  I can rise to the challenge
   ☐ b)  I might doubt that I really have the ability

**12**   During a break at work I would take the opportunity to:
   ☐ a)  chat with other people
   ☐ b)  have some time to myself

**13**  I prefer to:
- [ ] a) carry out actions in the way decided
- [ ] b) get agreement for a general idea

**14**  I would rather spend my time:
- [ ] a) learning a foreign language
- [ ] b) studying investment strategy

**15**  When there is an urgent problem it is best to:
- [ ] a) do it and deal with people's concerns later
- [ ] b) deal with people's concerns before doing it

**16**  'I thrive on pressure and tough challenges':
- [ ] a) Yes
- [ ] b) No

**17**  If I am with a group of people:
- [ ] a) I am usually the one who organizes things
- [ ] b) I am usually happy to do what someone else wants

**18**  I tend to agree that:
- [ ] a) there is a correct way of accomplishing a task
- [ ] b) if the result is satisfactory it does not matter how a task is accomplished

**19**  I would prefer to:
- [ ] a) discuss a novel
- [ ] b) repair a broken machine

**20**  I am more likely to deal with the difficulties a person has by:
- [ ] a) doing it myself
- [ ] b) listening to what other people say

**21**  When I take on difficult responsibilities or have to make decisions:
- [ ] a) I do not see them as burdens
- [ ] b) They can place a strain on me

**22**  When invited to a group activity:
- [ ] a) I am excited about being able to join in
- [ ] b) I regret that it will interrupt my plan

**23**  I tend to prefer to:
- [ ] a) check the details of what has to be done
- [ ] b) form a general idea of what has to be done

**24**  I am better at:
- ☐ a)  creating an abstract painting
- ☐ b)  drawing up a plan for a kitchen

**25**  In regard to the statement 'The end justifies the means':
- ☐ a)  I tend to agree
- ☐ b)  I tend to disagree

**26**  If asked to take on a responsibility that is new to me I think:
- ☐ a)  it would be humiliating to fail because I am not ready
- ☐ b)  I do not care about looking foolish, it is the only way to learn

**27**  I prefer to be with:
- ☐ a)  just one or two people
- ☐ b)  lots of people

**28**  If I am going to attend an important meeting or interview I:
- ☐ a)  leave it until I get there and see how things go
- ☐ b)  plan for what might happen as thoroughly as possible

**29**  I am more excited thinking about:
- ☐ a)  possible methods of space travel
- ☐ b)  finding a way towards spiritual awareness

**30**  People perform better when they are motivated by:
- ☐ a)  affection
- ☐ b)  fear

**31**  I sometimes think my views are less interesting or useful than those of others:
- ☐ a)  agree
- ☐ b)  disagree

**32**  When in a group I am:
- ☐ a)  one of the quietest
- ☐ b)  one of the loudest

**33**  Typically I:
- ☐ a)  rely on important things to occur to me
- ☐ b)  make a list of things to remember

**34**  I prefer to create something that is:
- ☐ a)  useful
- ☐ b)  beautiful

**35**  If asked whether I think people are trustworthy:
- ☐ a)  I tend to agree
- ☐ b)  I tend to disagree

**36**  I feel that for me it is:
- [ ] a) difficult to know in what way I can feel successful
- [ ] b) possible to experience feelings of success most of the time

**37**  When a group of people want somebody to take charge I am likely to:
- [ ] a) hold myself back
- [ ] b) push myself forward

**38**  Typically I like to:
- [ ] a) react to circumstances as they arise
- [ ] b) plan what I am going to do

**39**  I would find more value in studying:
- [ ] a) physics
- [ ] b) philosophy

**40**  Listening to the thoughts and feelings of everybody who is involved in a project:
- [ ] a) is valuable because it makes progress easier later on
- [ ] b) wastes valuable time when progress should be made

**41**  When asked to do something that has been beyond me thus far I am:
- [ ] a) doubtful whether I can live up to what people expect
- [ ] b) determined to do better than people expect

**42**  In communicating with a group of people about the same issue, I prefer to:
- [ ] a) write a letter or talk to them individually
- [ ] b) get them all together and talk to them

**43**  I think that:
- [ ] a) people realize what they have to do in their job when the moment is right for them
- [ ] b) unless people are clear about what their job is, nothing will get done properly

**44**  I tend to make up my mind by:
- [ ] a) weighing up the facts
- [ ] b) the impression I have gained

**45**  I would rather that my boss:
- [ ] a) allowed me to be aware of their personal difficulties
- [ ] b) did not bother me with their personal difficulties

**46** I find that self-doubt prevents me doing what I would like:
- ☐ a) Yes
- ☐ b) No

**47** I am inclined to:
- ☐ a) keep work relationships separate from leisure time
- ☐ b) meet people I work with out of work as well

**48** I would cope with worries or problems:
- ☐ a) by giving less time to unimportant matters
- ☐ b) through orderliness and efficiency

**49** If it were possible I would prefer to:
- ☐ a) witness how the universe began
- ☐ b) talk with an alien intelligence

**50** I believe that understanding people's attitudes and values:
- ☐ a) is essential when people are working together
- ☐ b) gets in the way of getting on with what they are working on

## Marking scheme

Place a tick by each one of the items below that corresponds with your answers. It does not matter whether the tick is against 'a' or 'b'. Add up the number of ticks in each column.

|        | | | | | |
|--------|------|------|------|------|------|
|        | **1** a) | **2** a) | **3** a) | **4** a) | **5** a) |
|        | **6** a) | **7** a) | **8** a) | **9** a) | **10** a) |
|        | **11** a) | **12** a) | **13** a) | **14** a) | **15** a) |
|        | **16** a) | **17** a) | **18** a) | **19** a) | **20** a) |
|        | **21** a) | **22** a) | **23** a) | **24** a) | **25** a) |
|        | **26** b) | **27** b) | **28** b) | **29** b) | **30** b) |
|        | **31** b) | **32** b) | **33** b) | **34** b) | **35** b) |
|        | **36** b) | **37** b) | **38** b) | **39** b) | **40** b) |
|        | **41** b) | **42** b) | **43** b) | **44** b) | **45** b) |
|        | **46** b) | **47** b) | **48** b) | **49** b) | **50** b) |
| Totals: | = | = | = | = | = |
|        | C | O | D | I | T |

Transfer your results on the CODIT test to page 111.

# How to Interpret and Use Your Personality

The five scores on the test are called the C, O, D, I and T scales. Each score ranges from 0 to 10. Remember, you can complete this section by a) using your own results on the test or by b) using the results obtained from the way in which other people see you. Bring your scores forward from the previous section and enter them below:

| _____ | _____ | _____ | _____ | _____ |
|:--------:|:--------:|:--------:|:--------:|:--------:|
| C | O | D | I | T |

Using a circle or cross, you can enter each of your scores into the personality chart on the next page. It helps to make the chart clearer by joining the scores with a line.

Chart of personality

|   |   |   |   |   | **C scale** |   |   |   |   |   |   |   |   |   |   |   |
|---|---|---|---|---|---|---|---|---|---|---|---|---|---|---|---|---|
| **A** | 0 | 1 | 2 | 3 | 4 | – | 5 | – | 6 | 7 | 8 | 9 | 10 | **C** |

|   |   |   |   |   | **O scale** |   |   |   |   |   |   |   |   |   |   |   |
|---|---|---|---|---|---|---|---|---|---|---|---|---|---|---|---|---|
| **S** | 0 | 1 | 2 | 3 | 4 | – | 5 | – | 6 | 7 | 8 | 9 | 10 | **O** |

|   |   |   |   |   | **D scale** |   |   |   |   |   |   |   |   |   |   |   |
|---|---|---|---|---|---|---|---|---|---|---|---|---|---|---|---|---|
| **R** | 0 | 1 | 2 | 3 | 4 | – | 5 | – | 6 | 7 | 8 | 9 | 10 | **D** |

|   |   |   |   |   | **I scale** |   |   |   |   |   |   |   |   |   |   |   |
|---|---|---|---|---|---|---|---|---|---|---|---|---|---|---|---|---|
| **F** | 0 | 1 | 2 | 3 | 4 | – | 5 | – | 6 | 7 | 8 | 9 | 10 | **I** |

|   |   |   |   |   | **T scale** |   |   |   |   |   |   |   |   |   |   |   |
|---|---|---|---|---|---|---|---|---|---|---|---|---|---|---|---|---|
| **E** | 0 | 1 | 2 | 3 | 4 | – | 5 | – | 6 | 7 | 8 | 9 | 10 | **T** |

## *Interpretation*

Each scale provides two descriptions depending upon whether your score on each scale ranges from 0 to 4 or from 6 to 10. Therefore, the five aspects of personality provide 10 descriptions in all. The first of these is the C scale, on which, for example, you will be coded C if your score is between 6 and 10, whilst you will be coded A if your score is between 0 and 4. Again, if your score on the O scale is 3, your code letter will be S, and so on with the other scales.

What happens if you have a score of 5? In this case you will have to decide for yourself whether, on balance, you tend more towards one description than the other. You will be able to make this decision more clearly when you have read what each of the scales is measuring. These are described below. The fact that your score is 5 suggests that you are balanced on this scale and might behave in either manner described, depending upon the circumstances, although your behaviour is unlikely to be extreme. You will have to bear this in mind when the interpretation of your personality becomes more detailed later on in the section. Clearly, the higher or lower the score on each scale, the more likely it is that the kind of behaviour described by the letter will be typical of you. A good way to get this matter clear is to ask another person (someone who knows you well) to complete the questionnaire for you. You may well have done this already by using method b) described at the beginning of the previous section.                ⅉ

## C scale

This is a general measure of how well you are able to cope with the various pressures and problems that arise in life and particularly at work.

**C scale**

**A**    0    1    2    3    4    –    5    –    6    7    8    9    10    **C**

Apprehensive
You tend to doubt yourself, wondering whether you can rise to new challenges. You are inclined to worry and may not take on all of which you are capable. You question yourself and are reluctant to be in a position where you may give a poor account of yourself or let others down. For the time being, avoid careers that involve uncertainty or continual, unreasonable pressure.

Your caution acts as a sensible means of protecting yourself from worry. Doing what you know you can reasonably manage or taking one small step at a time allows you to cope. It means that through the avoidance of risk you avoid making any great mistakes.

Confident
You are keen to take on those challenges that interest you. Even when these are difficult you are willing to have a go. You are not put off by fear of failure and the odd setback does not embarrass you long. Look for a career that is 'open ended' in the sense of providing new or different opportunities, not necessarily a completely new job, but one that offers new, challenging aspects.

Others may admire your approach to life, since you are so positive. You can be unrealistic, thinking you have the necessary abilities before you do.

Although you learn as you go along, you might have done better had you held back until

You are more capable than you give yourself credit for. People see your talents more clearly than you and are surprised that you do not project yourself more confidently. This dimension is not a permanent state of mind, so if you find a way to become confident you are almost bound to find that the other dimensions of personality change too.

you were more prepared. Your spontaneity will enable you to be a high achiever. You have a fundamental belief in yourself and what you can do that is entirely justified and you should have good fun in doing all of those things you want.

With experience you have probably learnt that you can achieve even more through allowing others to be involved with you.

## O scale

This is a scale that looks principally at the way you relate to people: do you want to be included with others a lot or a little? At one extreme you would want to spend almost all your time with others, whilst at the other you would want to work entirely on your own.

**O scale**

**S** 0 1 2 3 4 – 5 – 6 7 8 9 10 **O**

Solitary
Your personality is 'introverted', that is, you reflect upon what is happening to you, turning matters over in your mind. You are self-reliant and come up with solutions to issues by using your own resources. You like your own company or that of just one or very few others. Choose careers accordingly.

It can happen that the contribution you could make is

Outgoing
You have an 'extroverted' personality, that is, one that goes out and is active in doing things. Naturally gregarious, you will particularly enjoy interacting with others and achieving with and through them. You will want a career that brings you into contact with lots of people so that you can use social flair to make contacts and influence people.

not made apparent. You may be more talented than others, but what you can do is not communicated as you are not seen as a leader.

Alternatively, people are surprised that you seem resourceful, but do not participate. You can be perceived as over-serious or intolerant.

On the positive side, certain individuals may have experienced your caring side, both introverts and extroverts who recognize something deeper in you. Although often slow in making acquaintances, you can form attachments that are long lasting.

You may at times 'turn people off' through the sheer volume and power of your approach. You may be seen as insincere or manipulative. People may not immediately trust you as you appear to be over-friendly too soon or they suspect that you are 'out for yourself'.

Your social confidence is a great asset when it comes to coordinating or directing others. You are capable of arranging people and events. Because you have a talent for 'breaking the ice' socially you can effectively make contact with strangers and help them feel at ease and that they belong.

## D scale

This scale looks at the way you approach your work: do you focus upon order and structure or do you prefer to deal with matters in an impulsive and laissez-faire way?

**D scale**

**R**  0  1  2  3  4  –  5  –  6  7  8  9  10  **D**

Relaxed
You have a casual style that can be described as disorderly and unfocused. You may be seen as unbothered or that you take on too many things at once. You may seem to be

Detailed
In attending to what has to be done and approaching tasks in an orderly way you cement your own and others' efforts. You are essential in making sure that matters are properly finished

'flying by the seat of your pants'. The career that suits you best is one where you can focus upon ways of doing things – the strategic or longer, wider issues – rather than immediate, concrete problems.

Those aspects of you that are disorganized can make life very difficult for those dependent upon you. You can be perceived as keeping a team back. You may be offended that people leave you out of their schemes, but this is probably due to the fact that you let them down in the first place.

Your relaxed approach enables you to see the underlying structure or longer-term implications. You can also display a relaxed and tolerant manner with others that encourages them to work with you, especially on problems that are connected with ideas and possibilities. You can be exciting to work with.

without untidy 'loose ends'. You ensure that matters happen in the way intended so should look for a career in which you look at issues tactically, dealing with implementation of plans.

At times you can concentrate overmuch upon the orderliness of what you are doing to the extent that it really does not add any more to the issue. You may have 'overkilled' the issue or have ceased to 'see the wood for the trees'. People may see you as a little boring. They see you as holding them back due to the unnecessary small points you raise over minutiae.

Your careful preparation assists you in achieving often large and complex goals. Your orderliness can also permit others to find their own structure. You can often be seen as reliable and an essential member of a team without whom nothing would actually get done.

## I scale

This scale measures a preferred style: are you likely to be guided by feelings and impressions or do you like to establish evidence? This scale is not about creativity, though it has some correlation with a quantifying style versus an expressive one.

**I scale**

**F** 0 1 2 3 4 – 5 – 6 7 8 9 10 **I**

Factual

You think through problems in a logical way. Where there is uncertainty you look for facts. You are reassured when you can deal with concrete and objective reality. You like to deal with things that are measurable and can be made self-evident. You are suited to careers where the facts of the matter can be ascertained through measurement or through some means of agreed quality.

You may find that you have not developed some of the 'feeling side' of your nature. You may be perceived as unfeeling or even 'cold' because you appear to be overly focused upon numbers or 'things' and do not take emotions or values into account.

By being active and taking action where there is opportunity to create something definite you can be a real achiever. You can be particularly effective in producing something coherent or tangible that others can understand or apply in some practical way.

Intuitive

Your interest is in possibilities and the abstract. Conceptualization is more important than realization. You are sensitive to impressions and can make connections between seemingly disparate events or ideas. You are often suited to a career where you have a guiding or advisory responsibility because you can see the wider implications, particularly cultural or emotional issues.

At times your thinking may appear to be 'woolly' or imprecise. Experiencing the truth of an issue yourself is not the same as communicating it adequately to others, so you need to ensure that what you do is appropriate and actually wanted. If not, you may feel hurt and blame others for your feelings of rejection.

Through your insight you may produce something that others experience as uplifting or magical, making an impact either through something you create literally or in the relationship you develop between yourself and others.

## T scale

This scale measures the degree to which your objectives are concerned with what and how people achieve externally or the impact upon them internally. The orientation is tough and materialistic, or sensitive and spiritual.

**T scale**

**E**   0   1   2   3   4   –   5   –   6   7   8   9   10   **T**

Empathetic

Your response to decisions and to events is to perceive the implications for people and their lives. You believe in the potential of people, wanting them to be included and have responsibility. Your understanding of others' situations will bring out their best. You would enjoy a career in which you were able to support people and develop their potential, particularly in an organization where there is a commitment to involve people.

You may be seen as 'soft' or a 'do-gooder', so you are best giving help when it is asked for and refraining from intruding where it is not. It is possible to be unrealistic about people's intentions or to be 'taken in' and manipulated.

With the sensitivity that allows you to identify with others you can be the catalyst

Tough

Your objective is to achieve efficiently and quickly. You may have a vision of what it is possible to achieve and your talent is driving to attain it against all odds. You are particularly good at a career in a 'troubleshooting' position where immediate action is required to head off impending disaster. In such situations people are often willing to suspend the niceties simply in order to survive!

You can be seen as a 'tough' character, even as a bully. People may withhold information from you because they are frightened that you will dismiss or humiliate them, only wanting to 'hear what you want to hear'. Sometimes you hold on to a plan for too long because of stubbornness.

Your achievements can be outstanding when you are

that assists them to give of their best. You can be particularly valuable as a motivator by instinctively recognizing what will make people fulfilled.

'given your head' to do things your own way and where your decisions and methods do not require countersignature or approval.

Thus, your personality result can be described by five letters, for example, A O D I E or C S R F T or C O D F E, and so on. This is your personality code. Write your own 5 letters on the line below:

Personality code

_____

## *Basic behaviour descriptions*

As mentioned earlier, the C scale represents a 'modifier' of your behaviour, whilst the other scales provide core descriptions of your involvement with and impact on people, and your preferred habit and styles of working. These permit some fundamental analysis of your orientation and focus at work. You can use these to check whether the work you want is likely to suit your personality, or if you are in work already, how well your work is consistent with your personality. It is best to interpret for yourself what your results on the scales might mean in your own case. However, from the four scales here are some possibilities that frequently emerge:

1    How much you join in with people and how you do your work

|  | O – outgoing | S – solitary |
|---|---|---|
| **R – relaxed** | Involves people | Maintains 'status quo' |
| **D – detailed** | Focuses people | Organizes self |

2    How much you join in with people and your way of expression

|  | O – outgoing | S – solitary |
|---|---|---|
| **F – factual** | Works on facts with others | Works by self with facts |
| **I – intuitive** | Works with others on ideas | Works by self on ideas |

**3** How much you join in with people and your impact on people

|  | **O – outgoing** | **S – solitary** |
|---|---|---|
| **E – empathetic** | Supports people | Works for people |
| **T – tough** | Directs people | Takes action by self |

**4** Your impact upon people and how you do your work

|  | **E – empathetic** | **T – tough** |
|---|---|---|
| **R – relaxed** | Shares with people | Advises people |
| **D – detailed** | Assists people | Organizes people |

**5** Your impact upon people and your way of expression

|  | **E – empathetic** | **T – tough** |
|---|---|---|
| **F – factual** | Balances facts and feelings | Directs action on basis of fact |
| **I – intuitive** | Spiritual/creative | Directs creative endeavour |

**6** How you do your work and your way of expression

|  | **R – relaxed** | **D – detailed** |
|---|---|---|
| **F – factual** | Accepts situation | Organizes situation |
| **I – intuitive** | Gradual evolution | Structures evolution |

## Personality analysis chart

Your behaviour to people and your approach to your task are described by the last four letters of your personality code, thus providing 16 analyses. These are also affected, but not altered, by your first letter, either C or A. When the C scale is taken into account, this gives us 32 analyses. For convenience, your personality in relation to work is summed up in the following scheme:

| | | | |
|---|---|---|---|
| 1. C/A ODIT | 5. C/A ORIT | 9. C/A SDIT | 13. C/A SRIT |
| 2. C/A ODIE | 6. C/A ORIE | 10. C/A SDIE | 14. C/A SRIE |
| 3. C/A ODFT | 7. C/A ORFT | 11. C/A SDFT | 15. C/A SRFT |
| 4. C/A ODFE | 8. C/A ORFE | 12. C/A SDFE | 16. C/A SRFE |

Where you have a score of 5 on any scale it is possible that two of the above numbers might apply to you. For example, if your personality code was C O D F E, but your score on one of the scales, say, E was 5, then the analyses for C O D F T might equally be appropriate. You will have to see what meaning exists for you in the scales. The interpretation of personality and personality potential is complex, even, and elusive. The analyses provide only a limited interpretation; individuals can be very different due to their own circumstances, experience and understanding of the dimensions. If you do not perceive the analysis to be exactly you, do not reject it out of hand, but use it as a basis for self-exploration. Ask yourself whether there might be more truth in it than you might sometimes think or whether some parts apply to you in some circumstances and not others, or whether you could see that some other aspects not mentioned in the text might be true of you, and so on.

## *Analyses*

### 1.   C/A ODIT: 'a rescuer'

You like to be included with others and go out of your way to meet them. You like to work with people in a purposeful and goal-oriented way. You are likely to be seen as dynamic and determined. You might be seen as forceful with a strong, controlling style of leadership. You can be a force to be reckoned with as you can be both a source of ideas, but also exacting about the way things are put into practice. You are likely to be an achiever who, whilst adaptable and companionable, wants to achieve to the limit of your ability and will allow little to stand in your way. Your capacity for work and your social skill will probably take you into management, where you will enjoy directing others and tackling new and difficult problems.

If your confidence is high (C), it is likely that you will often succeed where others might have given up hope. You are therefore a good 'rescuer' of situations. If your confidence is lower (A), it may be wiser to remain longer within your job, not letting others, who are impressed with what you have done so far, persuade you to go on before you are ready.

## 2.    C/A ODIE: 'an agent for change'

You have a power and resourcefulness in relating to people. You understand people and their difficulties quickly, but also encourage their potential. People warm to you in turn as they recognize the fundamental sympathy you have for them and they will want to be involved with you in the projects you are likely to undertake. You like novelty and you can be inspired by opportunities, whilst at the same time you take a measured and careful look at what has to be done and the best way for it to be undertaken. You are suited to a career in which you can be part of building an organization.

Where your confidence is high (C) you will easily be recognized as a natural leader. The problem might arise in that people ask you to take on more and more responsibility. It is important to be able to extend yourself, but unwise to overload yourself, so if your confidence is low (A), find ways of reining back until you find the balance that you want.

## 3.    C/A ODFT: 'a producer'

Yours is a strong, resourceful character with a forceful and no-nonsense approach to the work situation. You mix with people readily, but are likely to have a driving manner that some will find motivating and others unnecessarily demanding. Certainly, you expect people to keep up with you. You are enthusiastic and an achiever. You like to work with others who are similarly motivated by hard work and success. When you find something you want to achieve, you are likely to apply yourself with doggedness and the energy to overcome or even disregard obstacles that get in your way. As you make it your business to know a great deal about what you are doing and prepare carefully, you will be perceived as being able to manage in a number of different areas.

Where your confidence is high (C) you will often set the direction for others to follow. Take care not to be impatient with those whose ideas are not as immediately focused upon the task as you. If your confidence is low (A), you may be better in a maintaining or slowly developing role as opposed to one where there could be rapid downturns or unpleasant surprises, since your liking to have control would be threatened in such circumstances.

## 4.   C/A ODFE: 'a negotiator'

You will have most scope in an organization that sees people as a valuable resource. You will then have the chance to fuse your sensitivity and social skills with your capacity for administration in a way that creates benefits for everybody who works together and for the organization as a whole. You are a person who will have 'an ear to the ground', and knowing what people are thinking and feeling will make you effective in negotiating with people and managing them appropriately. You could quite well be knowledgeable and with a sharp, legalistic turn of mind that will make you quite formidable to deal with. However, people will probably perceive you as less of an opponent than as someone who wants to work with them and for them for the common good. At the same time, you are not merely altruistic, but want to achieve in a way that demonstrates achievement, probably in business or other tangible ways.

Where your confidence is high (C) you will probably find yourself in a demanding job where your skills can be used in managing a large and wide range of people. Where it is low (A) it will be important to ensure that the organization you are in has a philosophy that is compatible with your own and also that the output, or product, is one that you can identify with. For example, you may find yourself more in tune with an organization concerned with production or other tangible things than with an organization concerned with, say, communications or the media. Much depends upon the size and the 'culture' of the company.

## 5.   C/A ORIT: 'using flair'

You are likely to display self-reliance and composure. At ease in most situations, there seems little you could not turn your mind to if you so desired. Without being unnecessarily forceful, you have definite views. Ideas come easily to you and you are capable of flowing from one issue to the next without difficulty. You will commonly be a leader when it comes to change and to finding ways to undertake projects in radical ways. You will flourish best within organizations that allow you to use flair and initiative. You could become bored and restless with a job that is routine. Usually, your ideas together with the easy way you have with people will enable you to work with others as a task director. You will like a creative environment where quick thinking is required and where you have to be 'quick on your feet'. Whilst good at relationships, you prefer people to deal with their own problems and not to bother you with personal matters that might get in the way of what it is you are creating.

Where your confidence is high (C) you would be expected to be in an unusually demanding 'leading edge' type of business. If you have (A), you could try to involve others more, for example letting them in on what you are thinking so that they can assist you more as opposed to continually looking to you for inspiration.

## 6.   C/A ORIE: 'open to ideas'

You have a quality that others will admire in you and make them want to know you. Potentially, there is an inner confidence and openness of mind that has a spiritual aspect. Characteristically, you are open to ideas and to people. You can see all sides of an argument, bringing an understanding and unbiased view that others will find useful in explaining and, perhaps, resolving their own conflicts. Without being at all forceful you will have a great impact upon others, who will often take the lead from you. If you are not in the right situation, you might frustrate people whose ultimate goals are more material or less people oriented than your own. You will therefore be ill at ease in an organization that is dismissive of people's personal or cultural values. No doubt you have established some guiding principles of philosophy that inform your life, so you work best in an organization that welcomes this.

If your confidence is high (C), you are probably already working in a way that suits you. You have the outlet or the contacts that make you feel that your efforts are having some real value in your own terms. Where your confidence is lower (A) there is probably an imperfect adjustment. This does not imply you should make any radical changes, particularly since you are unlikely to want to expose yourself to even more uncertainties, but you may be able to make some small critical adjustments so that you can achieve more of the qualitative work that you find to be most satisfying.

## 7.   C/A ORFT: 'law unto yourself'

You are of an extremely self-reliant type. Whilst you can mix with others easily, you are unlikely to be dependent. You like company and people like to be associated with you, even though you can be something of a 'law unto yourself'. You are suited to a position in which you have a good deal of freedom to do things your own way. Although you will be successful in making contacts and persuading others about what you can contribute, you do not like to be in a situation where others might slow you down. Doing things your way can be perceived as 'risky' since you are opportunistic and may leave things until the last moment. Generally, the clarity you possess about your own direction, together with the fact you are so well informed, will enable you to be an achiever. You can set the direction or goals for others, but may not have the tolerance to manage others on a day-to-day basis. As always, much depends upon the organization and its people.

With high confidence (C) you are probably regarded as a great resource by those who employ you or share in your success. If anything, you will probably be looking for a move in order to achieve even greater rewards. If you have a score that is (A) you may have overreached to the point where you were simply trying to keep far too many plates spinning! You are best advised to start again in a smaller way and this time recognize that even you have limitations, so try to stay within those, at least for more of the time!

## 8.   C/A ORFE: 'creates a positive atmosphere'

You have the ability to get to know others quickly and to obtain their confidence. Although perceived as capable and resourceful, you are regarded as an ally rather than a threat. In fact, you are often a natural confidante. Moreover, the practical way you have of weighing up problems and issues enables you to impart advice that is more than well meaning, but also sensible. There could be a danger that you sort out problems for people rather than allow them to do it themselves; you want to help and the solution is often quite clear to you. Where you have responsibility for others you are likely to create a happy and supportive team around you. Make sure you do not become over-involved in 'protecting' your associates from threats from outside it. Hopefully, you can create a positive working atmosphere in other parts of the organization. Generally, the way in which people work together and the work environment will be as important or even more important than the nature of the product or the work itself, so you need to be in an organization that is consistent with your values.

## 9. C/A SDIT: 'organized and expert'

You have clear ideas about how you want to lead your life. You do not necessarily force your views on others, although you can be surprisingly authoritative and categorical. You are well organized and self-sufficient. You are also likely to be knowledgeable, even quite learned in some cultural areas. You are probably most suited to a position in which you are something of an expert. This is because, although you might enjoy discussion and debate, you have probably established a procedure or have a view that is well informed. You allow yourself to be open to question, but probably defend your professional expertise. You are unlikely to enjoy getting too much involved in situations at work in which a sympathetic response might win people over or obtain their support. Therefore, the issues or principles you are dealing with may be more important to you than any individual. You may well have quite an intellectual approach to your work and therefore thrive best when you have the training that enables you to be recognized as an expert.

If you are also (C), you will be highly effective in an authoritative job that carries much responsibility since you will be able to make judgements without doubts about your personal capability. If you are (A), then you may be more suited to more of a 'back room' or advisory role where you are less exposed to personal criticism.

## 10. C/A SDIE: 'makes situations clear'

Although you are not a social type, people will like you because they know that your serious qualities are combined with a concern and understanding of them. You will be effective in 'reading situations' and clarifying these for others. Your perceptions in relation to people are keen and insightful. You are less good as a task manager than in a role that requires some coaxing or therapeutic support of others. As someone who seeks for explanations and rarely regards anything as a self-evident truth, you are likely to have developed a high regard for cultural values and attitudes. You are open-minded, but your mind is also likely to be incisive. You will enjoy work that allows you to contribute in a way that develops people and ideas in a qualitative way. Your work may well bring in aspects of creative endeavour and might also connect strongly with the caring professions.

If you have the letter (C), you are likely to be something of a campaigner on behalf of what you believe in. However, the fact that you have a 'cause' you take responsibility for might take you away from the direct contact with others that you are so good at. If you have the letter (A), you may enjoy working on a project or on behalf of others in something of a detached way where the emotional stresses are less extreme, for example relating to people on a one-to-one basis, rather than as a manager.

## 11.   C/A SDFT: 'applies knowledge'

You like to work in your own way with a minimum of hindrance from others. Although you will enjoy providing some sort of service or product that others will admire, respect or be grateful for, your preference is to have them leave the process up to you. No doubt you can be resourceful, since you tend to look to yourself for ideas. Often you will work out a competent approach to deal with problems. With your orderly and factual mind you could well be impressive as someone with the knowledge and expertise to make things work and get things done. You have clear opinions about many matters, but you may lack some insight into other people and what motivates them. If you find some emotional matters confusing, your tactic is probably to cope with these by ignoring them or by putting yourself into a position, say, where your responsibilities are technical as opposed to personal, where you do not have to deal with them. Therefore, you are probably most suited to a task-oriented or specialized type of career.

Where you also have (C) you are obviously pursuing the career before you enthusiastically. Operating on the basis of experience and attainments so far, your confidence will make you a significant contributor to the success of an organization, especially where the thrust of your work is on the technical side. If you have (A), then you would be best avoiding responsibilities where you think or have been told you ought to be effective, but where your fundamental disposition is at odds with what is required. For example, do not feel guilty if you are unsuccessful in a position requiring a softness of intuition and social skills – simply move into a job that is more suited to the strengths of your character.

## 12.   C/A SDFE: 'thoughtful'

In relating to people you are suited to a position in which you can provide an expert service as an insightful professional. This is because your thoughtfulness and sensitivity are very much appreciated by others who require considered, expert help from someone who also displays understanding and tolerance of their situation. People will also like your capability and efficiency. You not only respond to them, but you can also arrange matters for them in order that they receive some tangible help that will materially affect their lives. Although not an extrovert, your attention will often be focused upon people. Again, from a background that often has had a scientific or technical training of some kind, you will use your skills on behalf of others. Often you will be characterized as quietly efficient, whilst people will both depend upon you and like you.

If your confidence is shown in a (C), you would want a career that gives you a demanding managerial responsibility within your own career specialism. You will be a good, hard-working leader who, indeed, leads 'from the front'. If you have an (A), then you probably need to bide your time until you become assured of the underlying strength and potential of your character. Do not allow yourself to be imposed upon or be given a responsibility that will take you away from the quality of contact with others and ability to apply your own skills in a direct way in the service of others.

## 13.   C/A SRIT: 'independent'

You are suited to a career in which you can be self-reliant. Quite possibly you will want to follow your own urges and interests completely. If working with others, then you will like to have considerable independence. You may well show intolerance if things are not done your way, although you may be seen as somewhat casual in your responsibility towards them. Owing to the fact that you operate to your own schedule and your own imperatives, it is often best that those around you are not dependent upon you for immediate support, but that your contact or obligation to them is over a longer time frame or on a more flexible basis. There is no doubt that you can make valuable, necessary contributions to a team. Indeed, people may think that they 'cannot do without you' even though you can be infuriating to work with at times. Your value often lies in the ideation and inspiration you can generate. You are probably best suited to a fast-paced sector where development and achievement are rapid.

Where you are also (C) you will be something of a dynamic achiever. Be careful that you are not seen as someone who 'leaves the debris for others to clear up'. This can happen where you use your energy to make quick changes and then go on to the next task before setting up a structure that will carry on after you. If you are (A), then you may find more enjoyment and satisfaction in having someone around you who is capable of applying a steadying hand to what you do. Someone who can slow you down or direct you to some extent may have its frustrations but might prevent you from getting into desperate situations that could have been avoided.

## 14.   C/A SRIE: 'perceives the essential issue'

You will want to combine an interest in ideas and an affinity with people in your career. Often, you will be extremely well read and thus able to bring theory and practice to your relationships. It would not be at all surprising to find you in some kind of counselling, advisory or therapeutic role. Even where your organization is not specifically set up to develop, train or care for others, you will probably find yourself enjoying your work to the extent you are involved in one or all of these aspects. You are a good listener, but are also good at perceiving the nub of the issue. You will advise people in a way that is insightful as well as sympathetic to them individually. In fact, you have an ability to 'reach' people in a way that may well be emotionally or spiritually releasing for them.

Where you have (C) you will be able to demonstrate a maturity and balance that will enable you to pass on your skills to others. You can give people insights that will assist them in coping in what can be emotionally exhausting situations. If you have (A), you should probably avoid any demanding managerial or organization role that is inconsistent with the way you operate yourself, for example if you are asked to compromise your own values by senior members of an organization where their aims or methods are less altruistic than your own.

## 15.   C/A SRFT: 'task oriented'

As you do not seek out others for company very much and are task oriented you will generally prefer to set your own goals and get on with things in your own way. You are likely to get on with others well as you are not normally forceful in your relationships, although you might experience some schism where you are expected to work closely or interdependently. Then you might feel that one or the other of you was 'treading on toes'. Mostly, your enjoyment of your work as well as the contribution you make arises out of your being a capable, self-reliant operator. When given a task or, indeed, having identified the best procedure yourself, you carry it out in a thorough and capable way. It may be wise to inform people a little more about what you are doing; although you do not think such communication is necessary, it actually is, because people do not always realize (unless they know you well from experience) that you are in fact getting on with what you say you will do. Unless you make things plain, people may well see you as leaving things to the last moment, so when they are waiting for you because they need your effort before they can address their own part of the problem, you may well cause them some worry.

If you have (C), you will enjoy doing what you want, having found a situation, product or formula enabling you to work at what interests you when you want to. If you have (A), you should avoid situations that expose you to conflicts involving others that your own style makes it difficult to cope with. For example, you may be disadvantaged if expected to have the soft, subtle coping skills required in a diverse managerial role, because this will mean that the things you are better at have to be subordinated to them.

## 16.   C/A SRFE: 'a team builder'

You possess the potential to be a capable manager, even leader, of others provided that you are not expected to be very hard driving or enterprising. Lacking toughness and dispassion, you function best when you can work cooperatively with others. Seeing people as resourceful and welcoming what they can do, you will frequently get the best from them, creating a capable team around you in the process. A collegial environment suits your fairly shy as well as sensitive personality. In the normal course of things you can take on a great deal, particularly in supervising others, since you do not tend to worry overmuch and have a pretty common-sense view about what has to be done, how to do it and who is to do it. There can be a danger in stretching yourself too far, so that you may have to learn to say 'No' without fearing that you will upset people. People with this profile sometimes achieve less in terms of hierarchy or power than others expect, but this is because you do not possess the urge to achieve at the expense of alienating yourself from others or having to abandon the comfortable situation you make for yourself.

If you have (C), you are more likely to enjoy a demanding leadership responsibility and to have a career in which you are expected to communicate, often to large numbers of people or in new situations. If you have (A), you are more likely to be content with maintaining a familiar responsibility with people you develop a relationship with over time. Alternatively, you might have an advisory or 'consultancy' type of role where your contacts, whilst close, are temporary.

# PART THREE

# Career Analysis

# Introduction

The whole test, including all its parts, is very extensive indeed. Although you may wish to complete all sections, it is not necessary, as the test is designed so that you can spend your time concentrating on just those careers that are most likely to satisfy your interests.

In all parts of the test you are faced with a 'forced choice format', that is, you have to make a choice between one type of work and another. This means that your result will show which areas overall appeal to you most. This approach to testing is sometimes criticized on the basis that making a person choose between one or the other is unreal since, in real life, you would not be 'forced' to do either, just in the same way that nobody is going to 'force you to go to work'. Whilst this is no doubt true, the counter-argument is that most people will choose to go to work rather than choose not to. Therefore, the 'forced choice' method at least provides a positive direction based upon the principle of least unpleasant possibilities.

Most people will have at least some idea of what the different jobs mentioned involve, but where there is uncertainty or where you simply want to find out more, refer to careers publications (such as *The A–Z of Careers and Jobs* published by Kogan Page) in which you can find precise descriptions of the nature of the work, opportunities for progress, and so on.

You can decide beforehand on a particular approach to taking the test. There are two major approaches that are often taken and you can complete the test one or both of these ways if you want: 1) give a response based upon what interests you, irrespective of what you think about your competence or qualification; 2) respond to what interests you, but this time also considering what you think is actually possible for you based upon your real or anticipated skills and attainments.

In summary, the tests included in this book are intended to be a means by which you can discover more about yourself, how you compare with others and the type of career for which your aptitudes, personality and motivation might suit you. It usually follows that the discovery of potential leads on to the development of new interests and a fuller personal realization.

# Career Analysis Test (CAT)

This is a test containing a number of sub-tests, each of which finds out how much you are attracted by different types of work activity. You are given a sentence and you have to choose the activity that appeals to you. You must choose *only one* of the activities even though it might be difficult because both are equally attractive.

Of the two alternative activities you are given, both are equally 'good' or 'correct'. Neither is 'right' or 'wrong'. Please indicate the statement that appeals more. It is best to mark your answer with a pencil so that you can erase it if you change your mind. Simply respond to the test, asking yourself which of the activities appeals to you.

This test is not timed. Start when you are ready.

## *CAT Part 1*

The object of Part 1 is to establish areas of work that can be looked at in more detail in Part 2.

In each case, underline the one you prefer from each pair in response to the statement: 'I would like work involving. . .':

1  A) words or communication
   B) music or art

2  B) music or art
   C) helping or teaching

3  C) helping or teaching
   D) buying or selling

4  D) buying or selling
   E) administration or accountancy

5  E) administration or accountancy
   F) science or technology

6  F) science or technology
   G) activity or outdoors

7  G) activity or outdoors
   H) manufacturing or construction

8  A) words or communication
   C) helping or teaching

9  B) music or art
   D) buying or selling

10  C) helping or teaching
   E) administration or accountancy

11  D) buying or selling
   F) science or technology

12  E) administration or accountancy
   G) activity or outdoors

13  F) science or technology
   H) manufacturing or construction

14  A) words or communication
   D) buying or selling

15  B) music or art
   E) administration or accountancy

16  C) helping or teaching
   F) science or technology

17  D)  buying or selling
    G)  activity or outdoors
19  A)  words or communication
    E)  administration or accountancy
21  C)  helping or teaching
    G)  activity or outdoors
23  A)  words or communication
    F)  science or technology
25  C)  helping or teaching
    H)  manufacturing or construction
27  B)  music or art
    H)  manufacturing or construction

18  E)  administration or accountancy
    H)  manufacturing or construction
20  B)  music or art
    F)  science or technology
22  D)  buying or selling
    H)  manufacturing or construction
24  B)  music or art
    G)  activity or outdoors
26  A)  words or communication
    G)  activity or outdoors
28  A)  words or communication
    H)  manufacturing or  construction

## CAT Part 1    Marking scheme

Count the number of times you have underlined each of the letters A to H. The maximum is seven in each case. Write your score below:

| ___ | ___ | ___ | ___ | ___ | ___ | ___ | ___ |
|-----|-----|-----|-----|-----|-----|-----|-----|
| A   | B   | C   | D   | E   | F   | G   | H   |

Your highest score(s) show your preferred areas of working, thus indicating the most profitable categories to explore in Part 2. Each area from Part 1 corresponds to a category number in Part 2; A is 1, B is 2, and so on.

# CAT Part 2

The object of Part 2 is to establish work activities within each area that interest you the most. Where you are unsure what is actually involved in a form of work you can refer to a book such as *Occupations*, published by COIC, which can be found in a library.

## CAT Part 2, Category 1    Words or communication

In each case, underline the one you prefer from each pair in response to the statement: 'I would like work involving. . .':

| | |
|---|---|
| 1 A) journalism or writing | 2 B) publishing |
| B) publishing | C) museum exhibiting |
| 3 C) museum exhibiting | 4 D) library information |
| D) library information | E) archaeology |
| 5 E) archaeology | 6 F) interpreting or translation |
| F) interpreting or translation | G) acting |
| 7 G) acting | 8 H) broadcasting production/research |
| H) broadcasting production/research | I) legal advice |
| 9 A) journalism or writing | 10 B) publishing |
| C) museum exhibiting | D) library information |
| 11 C) museum exhibiting | 12 D) library information |
| E) archaeology | F) interpreting or translation |
| 13 E) archaeology | 14 F) interpreting or translation |
| G) acting | H) broadcasting production/research |
| 15 G) acting | 16 A) journalism or writing |
| I) legal advice | D) library information |
| 17 B) publishing | 18 C) museum exhibiting |
| E) archaeology | F) interpreting or translation |
| 19 D) library information | 20 E) archaeology |
| G) acting | H) broadcasting production/research |
| 21 F) interpreting or translation | 22 A) journalism or writing |
| I) legal advice | E) archaeology |
| 23 B) publishing | 24 C) museum exhibiting |
| F) interpreting or translation | G) acting |
| 25 D) library information | 26 E) archaeology |
| H) broadcasting production/research | I) legal advice |
| 27 A) journalism or writing | 28 B) publishing |
| F) interpreting or translation | G) acting |
| 29 C) museum exhibiting | 30 D) library information |
| H) broadcasting production/research | I) legal advice |
| 31 A) journalism or writing | 32 B) publishing |
| G) acting | H) broadcasting production/research |
| 33 C) museum exhibiting | 34 A) journalism or writing |
| I) legal advice | H) broadcasting production/research |
| 35 B) publishing | 36 A) journalism or writing |
| I) legal advice | I) legal advice |

# CAT Part 2, Category 1    Words or communication
# Marking scheme

Count the number of times you have underlined each of the letters A to I. The maximum is eight in each case. Write your score below:

| A | B | C | D | E | F | G | H | I |
|---|---|---|---|---|---|---|---|---|

Your highest score(s) show your preferred type of work in Category 1. Transfer your highest score in this category to page 152.

## CAT Part 2, Category 2    Music or art

In each case, underline the one you prefer from each pair in response to the statement: 'I would like work involving. . .':

1  A) musician or music teacher
   B) dancer
3  C) camera operator
   D) fashion model
5  E) beautician or hairdresser
   F) graphic designer or illustrator
7  G) design of textiles or fashion
   H) interior design
9  I) photography
   J) tailor or dressmaker
11  A) musician or music teacher
   C) camera operator
13  C) camera operator
   E) beautician or hairdresser
15  E) beautician or hairdresser
   G) design of textiles or fashion
17  G) design of textiles or fashion
   I) photography
19  I) photography
   K) upholsterer or polisher
21  B) dancer
   E) beautician or hairdresser
23  D) fashion model
   G) design of textiles or fashion
25  F) graphic designer or illustrator
   I) photography
27  H) interior design
   K) upholsterer or polisher
29  B) dancer
   F) graphic designer or illustrator
31  D) fashion model
   H) interior design

2  B) dancer
   C) camera operator
4  D) fashion model
   E) beautician or hairdresser
6  F) graphic designer or illustrator
   G) design of textiles or fashion
8  H) interior design
   I) photography
10  J) tailor or dressmaker
   K) upholsterer or polisher
12  B) dancer
   D) fashion model
14  D) fashion model
   F) graphic designer or illustrator
16  F) graphic designer or illustrator
   H) interior design
18  H) interior design
   J) tailor or dressmaker
20  A) musician or music teacher
   D) fashion model
22  C) camera operator
   F) graphic designer or illustrator
24  E) beautician or hairdresser
   H) interior design
26  G) design of textiles or fashion
   J) tailor or dressmaker
28  A) musician or music teacher
   E) beautician or hairdresser
30  C) camera operator
   G) design of textiles or fashion
32  E) beautician or hairdresser
   I) photography

33 F) graphic designer or illustrator
   J) tailor or dressmaker
35 A) musician or music teacher
   F) graphic designer or illustrator
37 C) camera operator
   H) interior design
39 E) beautician or hairdresser
   J) tailor or dressmaker
41 A) musician or music teacher
   G) design of textiles or fashion
43 C) camera operator
   I) photography
45 E) beautician or hairdresser
   K) upholsterer or polisher
47 B) dancer
   I) photography
49 D) fashion model
   K) upholsterer or polisher
51 B) dancer
   J) tailor or dressmaker
53 A) musician or music teacher
   J) tailor or dressmaker
55 A) musician or music teacher
   K) upholsterer or polisher

34 G) design of textiles or fashion
   K) upholsterer or polisher
36 B) dancer
   G) design of textiles or fashion
38 D) fashion model
   I) photography
40 F) graphic designer or illustrator
   K) upholsterer or polisher
42 B) dancer
   H) interior design
44 D) fashion model
   J) tailor or dressmaker
46 A) musician or music teacher
   H) interior design
48 C) camera operator
   J) tailor or dressmaker
50 A) musician or music teacher
   I) photography
52) C) camera operator
   K) upholsterer or polisher
54 B) dancer
   K) upholsterer or polisher

## CAT Part 2, Category 2    Music or art
## Marking scheme

Count the number of times you have underlined each of the letters A to K. The maximum is 10 in each case. Write your score below:

  A    B    C    D    E    F    G    H    I    J    K

Your highest score(s) show your preferred type of work. Transfer your highest score to page 153 in Category 2.

## CAT Part 2, Category 3    Helping or teaching

In each case, underline the one you prefer from each pair in response to the statement: 'I would like work involving…':

1  A) personnel or training
   B) nursing
3  C) medical therapist or radiographer
   D) complementary medicine
5  E) social work
   F) probation work
7  G) nursery or infant work
   H) employment or career work
9  I) youth or community work
   J) psychology
11 K) police or prison service
   L) teaching
13 B) nursing
   D) complementary medicine
15 D) complementary medicine
   F) probation work
17 F) probation work
   H) employment or career work
19 H) employment or career work
   J) psychology
21 J) psychology
   L) teaching
23 B) nursing
   E) social work
25 D) complementary medicine
   G) nursery or infant work
27 F) probation work
   I) youth or community work
29 H) employment or career work
   K) police or prison service
31 A) personnel or training
   E) social work
33 C) medical therapist or radiographer
   G) nursery or infant work
35 E) social work
   I) youth or community work
37 G) nursery or infant work
   K) police or prison service
39 A) personnel or training
   F) probation work
41 C) medical therapist or radiographer
   H) employment or career work

2  B) nursing
   C) medical therapist or radiographer
4  D) complementary medicine
   E) social work
6  F) probation work
   G) nursery or infant work
8  H) employment or career work
   I) youth or community work
10 J) psychology
   K) police or prison service
12 A) personnel or training
   C) medical therapist or radiographer
14 C) medical therapist or radiographer
   E) social work
16 E) social work
   G) nursery or infant work
18 G) nursery or infant work
   I) youth or community work
20 I) youth or community work
   K) police or prison service
22 A) personnel or training
   D) complementary medicine
24 C) medical therapist or radiographer
   F) probation work
26 E) social work
   H) employment or career work
28 G) nursery or infant work
   J) psychology
30 I) youth or community work
   L) teaching
32 B) nursing
   F) probation work
34 D) complementary medicine
   H) employment or career work
36 F) probation work
   J) psychology
38 H) employment or career work
   L) teaching
40 B) nursing
   G) nursery or infant work
42 D) complementary medicine
   I) youth or community work

43 E) social work      44 F) probation work
   J) psychology        K) police or prison service
45 G) nursery or infant work    46 A) personnel or training
   L) teaching          G) nursery or infant work
47 B) nursing           48 C) medical therapist or radiographer
   H) employment or career work    I) youth or community work
49 D) complementary medicine   50 E) social work
   J) psychology        K) police or prison service
51 F) probation work      52 A) personnel or training
   L) teaching          H) employment or career work
53 B) nursing           54 C) medical therapist or radiographer
   I) youth or community work    J) psychology
55 D) complementary medicine   56 E) social work
   K) police or prison service    L) teaching
57 A) personnel or training    58 B) nursing
   I) youth or community work    J) psychology
59 C) medical therapist or radiographer   60 D) complementary medicine
   K) police or prison service    L) teaching
61 A) personnel or training    62 B) nursing
   J) psychology        K) police or prison service
63 C) medical therapist or radiographer   64 A) personnel or training
   L) teaching          K) police or prison service
65 B) nursing           66 A) personnel or training
   L) teaching          L) teaching

## CAT Part 2, Category 3    Helping or teaching Marking scheme

Count the number of times you have underlined each of the letters A to L. The maximum is 11 in each case. Write your score below:

A    B    C    D    E    F    G    H    I    J    K    L

Your highest score(s) show your preferred type of work in Category 3. Transfer your highest score to page 154.

## CAT Part 2, Category 4    Buying or selling

In each case, underline the one you prefer from each pair in response to the statement: 'I would like work involving. . .':

1  A)  marketing
   B)  advertising
3  C)  retail sales
   D)  public relations
5  E)  travelling sales representative
   F)  buying or purchase agent
7  G)  own business
   H)  shop franchise or public house
9  B)  advertising
   D)  public relations
11 D)  public relations
   F)  buying or purchase agent
13 F)  buying or purchase agent
   H)  shop franchise or public house
15 B)  advertising
   E)  travelling sales representative
17 D)  public relations
   G)  own business
19 A)  marketing
   E)  travelling sales representative
21 C)  retail sales
   G)  own business
23 A)  marketing
   F)  buying or purchase agent
25 C)  retail sales
   H)  shop franchise or public house
27 B)  advertising
   H)  shop franchise or public house

2  B)  advertising
   C)  retail sales
4  D)  public relations
   E)  travelling sales representative
6  F)  buying or purchase agent
   G)  own business
8  A)  marketing
   C)  retail sales
10 C)  retail sales
   E)  travelling sales representative
12 E)  travelling sales representative
   G)  own business
14 A)  marketing
   D)  public relations
16 C)  retail sales
   F)  buying or purchase agent
18 E)  travelling sales representative
   H)  shop franchise or public house
20 B)  advertising
   F)  buying or purchase agent
22 D)  public relations
   H)  shop franchise or public house
24 B)  advertising
   G)  own business
26 A)  marketing
   G)  own business
28 A)  marketing
   H)  shop franchise or public house

# CAT Part 2, Category 4   Buying or selling
Marking scheme

Count the number of times you have underlined each of the letters A to H. The maximum is seven in each case. Write your score below:

| A | B | C | D | E | F | G | H |
|---|---|---|---|---|---|---|---|
| ___ | ___ | ___ | ___ | ___ | ___ | ___ | ___ |

Your highest score(s) show your preferred type of work in Category 4. Transfer your highest score to page 155.

# CAT Part 2, Category 5    Administration or accountancy

In each case, underline the one you prefer from each pair in response to the statement: 'I would like work involving. . .':

1  A)  civil, local or health service
   B)  post office work or secretarial
3  C)  accounting or auditing
   D)  health and safety work
5  E)  travel or tourism
   F)  legal executive or court services
7  G)  banking or building society work
   H)  insurance or stock exchange
9  I)  housing management
   J)  planning or surveying
11 B)  post office work or secretarial
   D)  health and safety work
13 D)  health and safety work
   F)  legal executive or court services
15 F)  legal executive or court services
   H)  insurance or stock exchange
17 H)  insurance or stock exchange
   J)  planning or surveying
19 B)  post office work or secretarial
   E)  travel or tourism
21 D)  health and safety work
   G)  banking or building society work
23 F)  legal executive or court services
   I)  housing management
25 A)  civil, local or health service
   E)  travel or tourism
27 C)  accounting or auditing
   G)  banking or building society work
29 E)  travel or tourism
   I)  housing management
31 A)  civil, local or health service
   F)  legal executive or court services
33 C)  accounting or auditing
   H)  insurance or stock exchange
35 E)  travel or tourism
   J)  planning or surveying
37 B)  post office work or secretarial
   H)  insurance or stock exchange

2  B)  post office work or secretarial
   C)  accounting or auditing
4  D)  health and safety work
   E)  travel or tourism
6  F)  legal executive or court services
   G)  banking or building society work
8  H)  insurance or stock exchange
   I)  housing management
10 A)  civil, local or health service
   C)  accounting or auditing
12 C)  accounting or auditing
   E)  travel or tourism
14 E)  travel or tourism
   G)  banking or building society work
16 G)  banking or building society work
   I)  housing management
18 A)  civil, local or health service
   D)  health and safety work
20 C)  accounting or auditing
   F)  legal executive or court services
22 E)  travel or tourism
   H)  insurance or stock exchange
24 G)  banking or building society work
   J)  planning or surveying
26 B)  post office work or secretarial
   F)  legal executive or court services
28 D)  health and safety work
   H)  insurance or stock exchange
30 F)  legal executive or court services
   J)  planning or surveying
32 B)  post office work or secretarial
   G)  banking or building society work
34 D)  health and safety work
   I)  housing management
36 A)  civil, local or health service
   G)  banking or building society work
38 C)  accounting or auditing
   I)  housing management

39 D)  health and safety work
　　J)  planning or surveying
41 B)  post office work or secretarial
　　I)  housing management
43 A)  civil, local or health service
　　I)  housing management
45 A)  civil, local or health service
　　J)  planning or surveying

40 A)  civil, local or health service
　　H)  insurance or stock exchange
42 C)  accounting or auditing
　　J)  planning or surveying
44 B)  post office work or secretarial
　　J)  planning or surveying

## CAT Part 2, Category 5　Administration or accountancy Marking scheme

Count the number of times you have underlined each of the letters A to J. The maximum is nine in each case. Write your score below:

A　　B　　C　　D　　E　　F　　G　　H　　I　　J

Your highest score (s) show your preferred type of work in Category 5. Transfer your highest score to page 156.

## CAT Part 2, Category 6　Science or technology

In each case, underline the one you prefer from each pair in response to the statement: 'I would like work involving. . .':

1 A)  electronics or computer hardware
　　B)  software or web programming
3 C)  environmental health
　　D)  statistics or econometrics
5 E)  medicine or dentistry
　　F)  pharmacy or chemistry
7 G)  ophthalmic or medical technology
　　H)  food science or dietetics
9 I)  materials or earth sciences
　　J)  engineering
11 K)  veterinary surgery
　　L)  pilot or air control
13 B)  software or web programming
　　D)  statistics or econometrics

2 B)  software or web programming
　　C)  environmental health
4 D)  statistics or econometrics
　　E)  medicine or dentistry
6 F)  pharmacy or chemistry
　　G)  ophthalmic or medical technology
8 H)  food science or dietetics
　　I)  materials or earth sciences
10 J)  engineering
　　K)  veterinary surgery
12 A)  electronics or computer hardware
　　C)  environmental health
14 C)  environmental health
　　E)  medicine or dentistry

15 D) statistics or econometrics

F) pharmacy or chemistry

17 F) pharmacy or chemistry

H) food science or dietetics

19 H) food science or dietetics

J) engineering

21 J) engineering

L) pilot or air control

23 B) software or web programming

E) medicine or dentistry

25 D) statistics or econometrics

G) ophthalmic or medical technology

27 F) pharmacy or chemistry

I) materials or earth sciences

29 H) food science or dietetics

K) veterinary surgery

31 A) electronics or computer hardware

E) medicine or dentistry

33 C) environmental health

G) ophthalmic or medical technology

35 E) medicine or dentistry

I) materials or earth sciences

37 G) ophthalmic or medical technology

K) veterinary surgery

39 A) electronics or computer hardware

F) pharmacy or chemistry

41 C) environmental health

H) food science or dietetics

43 E) medicine or dentistry

J) engineering

45 G) ophthalmic or
medical technology

L) pilot or air control

47 B) software or web programming

H) food science or dietetics

49 D) statistics or econometrics

J) engineering

51 F) pharmacy or chemistry

L) pilot or air control

53 B) software or web programming

I) materials or earth sciences

16 E) medicine or dentistry

G) ophthalmic or medical technology

18 G) ophthalmic or medical technology

I) materials or earth sciences

20 I) materials or earth sciences

K) veterinary surgery

22 A) electronics or computer hardware

D) statistics or econometrics

24 C) environmental health

F) pharmacy or chemistry

26 E) medicine or dentistry

H) food science or dietetics

28 G) ophthalmic or medical technology

J) engineering

30 I) materials or earth sciences

L) pilot or air control

32 B) software or web programming

F) pharmacy or chemistry

34 D) statistics or econometrics

H) food science or dietetics

36 F) pharmacy or chemistry

J) engineering

38 H) food science or dietetics

L) pilot or air control

40 B) software or web programming

G) ophthalmic or medical technology

42 D) statistics or econometrics

I) materials or earth sciences

44 F) pharmacy or chemistry

K) veterinary surgery

46 A) electronics or computer
hardware

G) ophthalmic or medical technology

48 C) environmental health

I) materials or earth sciences

50 E) medicine or dentistry

K) veterinary surgery

52 A) electronics or computer hardware

H) food science or dietetics

54 C) environmental health

J) engineering

55 D) statistics or econometrics
   K) veterinary surgery
56 E) medicine or dentistry
   L) pilot or air control
57 A) electronics or computer hardware
   I) materials or earth sciences
58 B) software or web programming
   J) engineering
59 C) environmental health
   K) veterinary surgery
60 D) statistics or econometrics
   L) pilot or air control
61 A) electronics or computer hardware
   J) engineering
62 B) software or web programming
   K) veterinary surgery
63 C) environmental health
   L) pilot or air control
64 A) electronics or computer hardware
   K) veterinary surgery
65 B) software or web programming
   L) pilot or air control
66 A) electronics or computer hardware
   L) pilot or air control

## CAT Part 2, Category 6  Science or technology Marking scheme

Count the number of times you have underlined each of the letters A to L. The maximum is 11 in each case. Write your score below:

__  __  __  __  __  __  __  __  __  __  __

A  B  C  D  E  F  G  H  I  J  K  L

Your highest score(s) show your preferred type of work in Category 6. Transfer your highest score to page 157.

## CAT Part 2, Category 7  Activity or outdoors

In each case, underline the one you prefer from each pair in response to the statement: 'I would like work involving. . .':

1 A) armed forces or security
   B) sport or leisure
2 B) sport or leisure
   C) bar, restaurant or kitchen work
3 C) bar, restaurant or kitchen work
   D) refuse, windows and cleaning
4 D) refuse, windows and cleaning
   E) ambulance or fire service
5 E) ambulance or fire service
   F) driving or traffic control
6 F) driving or traffic control
   G) farm, horticulture or animal work
7 G) farm, horticulture or animal work
   H) forestry, parks or conservation
8 H) forestry, parks or conservation
   I) materials handling or funeral work
9 I) materials handling or funeral work
   J) porter or hospital services
10 A) armed forces or security
   C) bar, restaurant or kitchen work

11 B) sport or leisure
   D) refuse, windows and cleaning
13 D) refuse, windows and cleaning
   F) driving or traffic control
15 F) driving or traffic control
   H) forestry, parks or conservation
17 H) forestry, parks or conservation
   J) porter or hospital services
19 B) sport or leisure
   E) ambulance or fire service
21 D) refuse, windows and cleaning
   G) farm, horticulture or animal work
23 F) driving or traffic control
   I) materials handling or funeral work
25 A) armed forces or security
   E) ambulance or fire service
27 C) bar, restaurant or kitchen work
   G) farm, horticulture or animal work
29 E) ambulance or fire service
   I) materials handling or funeral work
31 A) armed forces or security
   F) driving or traffic control
33 C) bar, restaurant or kitchen work
   H) forestry, parks or conservation
35 E) ambulance or fire service
   J) porter or hospital services
37 B) sport or leisure
   H) forestry, parks or conservation
39 D) refuse, windows and cleaning
   J) porter or hospital services
41 B) sport or leisure
   I) materials handling or funeral work
43 A) armed forces or security
   I) materials handling or funeral work
45 A) armed forces or security
   J) porter or hospital services

12 C) bar, restaurant or kitchen work
   E) ambulance or fire service
14 E) ambulance or fire service
   G) farm, horticulture or animal work
16 G) farm, horticulture or animal work
   I) materials handling or funeral work
18 A) armed forces or security
   D) refuse, windows and cleaning
20 C) bar, restaurant or kitchen work
   F) driving or traffic control
22 E) ambulance or fire service
   H) forestry, parks or conservation
24 G) farm, horticulture or animal work
   J) porter or hospital services
26 B) sport or leisure
   F) driving or traffic control
28 D) refuse, windows and cleaning
   H) forestry, parks or conservation
30 F) driving or traffic control
   J) porter or hospital services
32 B) sport or leisure
   G) farm, horticulture or animal work
34 D) refuse, windows and cleaning
   I) materials handling or funeral work
36 A) armed forces or security
   G) farm, horticulture or animal work
38 C) bar, restaurant or kitchen work
   I) materials handling or funeral work
40 A) armed forces or security
   H) forestry, parks or conservation
42 C) bar, restaurant or kitchen work
   J) porter or hospital services
44 B) sport or leisure
   J) porter or hospital services

# CAT Part 2, Category 7   Activity or outdoors Marking scheme

Count the number of times you have underlined each of the letters A to J. The maximum is nine in each case. Write your score below:

| A | B | C | D | E | F | G | H | I | J |
|---|---|---|---|---|---|---|---|---|---|
| — | — | — | — | — | — | — | — | — | — |

Your highest score(s) show your preferred type of work in Category 7. Transfer your highest score to page 159.

## CAT Part 2, Category 8   Manufacturing or construction

In each case, underline the one you prefer from each pair in response to the statement: 'I would like work involving. . .':

1 A) using machines or manufacturing
   B) vehicle repair or maintenance
3 C) telecoms or service engineering
   D) food preparation
5 E) making textiles or furniture
   F) printing operations
7 G) ironwork or building crafts
   H) oil, highways and construction
9 B) vehicle repair or maintenance
   D) food preparation
11 D) food preparation
   F) printing operations
13 F) printing operations
   H) oil, highways and construction
15 B) vehicle repair or maintenance
   E) making textiles or furniture
17 D) food preparation
   G) ironwork or building crafts
19 A) using machines or manufacturing
   E) making textiles or furniture
21 C) telecoms or service engineering
   G) ironwork or building crafts
23 A) using machines or manufacturing
   F) printing operations
25 C) telecoms or service engineering
   H) oil, highways and construction
27 B) vehicle repair or maintenance
   H) oil, highways and construction

2 B) vehicle repair or maintenance
   C) telecoms or service engineering
4 D) food preparation
   E) making textiles or furniture
6 F) printing operations
   G) ironwork or building crafts
8 A) using machines or manufacturing
   C) telecoms or service engineering
10 C) telecoms or service engineering
   E) making textiles or furniture
12 E) making textiles or furniture
   G) ironwork or building crafts
14 A) using machines or manufacturing
   D) food preparation
16 C) telecoms or service engineering
   F) printing operations
18 E) making textiles or furniture
   H) oil, highways and construction
20 B) vehicle repair or maintenance
   F) printing operations
22 D) food preparation
   H) oil, highways and construction
24 B) vehicle repair or maintenance
   G) ironwork or building crafts
26 A) using machines or manufacturing
   G) ironwork or building crafts
28 A) using machines or manufacturing
   H) oil, highways and construction

## CAT Part 2, Category 8    Manufacturing or construction Marking scheme

Count the number of times you have underlined each of the letters A to H. The maximum is seven in each case. Write your score below:

| A | B | C | D | E | F | G | H |
|---|---|---|---|---|---|---|---|
| ___ | ___ | ___ | ___ | ___ | ___ | ___ | ___ |

Your highest score(s) show your preferred type of work in Category 8. Transfer your highest score to page 160.

# Directing Your Interests

The previous chapter presented you with a comprehensive pro-gramme of tests in order to analyse your work interests. The results should assist you to define your career in a meaningful and reward-ing way. The entire programme of sub-tests is a daunting task so that it is quite possible that you have not completed them all. That does not matter, as you may not need all of the test results to find what suits you best. But, if you find this chapter makes you feel you would benefit from filling out the picture by taking more of the sub-tests, you can always go back and do so.

Place your scores from CAT Part 1 (pages 134–35), which you completed in the previous section into the Areas of interest chart, below. Mark your score on each area with a tick, circle or cross, then join up the points.

Areas of interest chart

| | | | | | | | | |
|---|---|---|---|---|---|---|---|---|
| A | 0 | 1 | 2 | 3 | 4 | 5 | 6 | 7 |
| B | 0 | 1 | 2 | 3 | 4 | 5 | 6 | 7 |
| C | 0 | 1 | 2 | 3 | 4 | 5 | 6 | 7 |
| D | 0 | 1 | 2 | 3 | 4 | 5 | 6 | 7 |
| E | 0 | 1 | 2 | 3 | 4 | 5 | 6 | 7 |
| F | 0 | 1 | 2 | 3 | 4 | 5 | 6 | 7 |
| G | 0 | 1 | 2 | 3 | 4 | 5 | 6 | 7 |
| H | 0 | 1 | 2 | 3 | 4 | 5 | 6 | 7 |

A   words or communication
B   music or art
C   helping or teaching
D   buying or selling
E   administration or accountancy
F   science or technology
G   activity or outdoors
H   manufacturing or construction

A score of three in the chart is an average score. If you have results around this level, then the implication is that you are probably indifferent to most of the careers that would be contained within this category. At the same time, it is worth bearing in mind that it is possible that there may be a career within a category that contains an appeal for you, which is why it can be worth having a go at all the categories even though one of them appears to have no immediate attraction. Scores less than average indicate areas of clear rejection, although again the same qualification could be made as to the possibility that one of these areas might contain a single career that appeals to you. Again, the matter can only be settled by working exhaustively through all the tests.

Where you have high scores – five, six or seven – then you have distinguished the most likely areas in which you will find the career that suits you best. Where there is just a single high score the matter is even clearer. However, most people obtain two or more high score areas. Though you should look at the highest score first, it is then necessary to ask yourself how you might be able to 'put together' the different areas of interest that might have emerged. In fact, most careers are like this: they contain a number of elements and sometimes 'cross over' or 'join up' the areas that have been classified here. For example, legal work might be classified under the area of 'words or communication', but many solicitors would see their work as being more involved with 'administration or accountancy', whilst others may see a stronger connection with 'helping or teaching'; much depends upon the specific nature of the job, the business or the organization for which they work. The same is true for many careers. It also frequently happens that a person does not need to change their job completely to obtain more job satisfaction, but to realign their work in order to be more involved in the areas that have an appeal to them.

The test of preferred career areas, although very brief, is a complex test and it will repay you to think through the results thoroughly. Besides the issues of how to put together your preferred choices, there are other questions that it can be useful to ask yourself, for example: 'On what basis am I rejecting some areas and not others? Do I think my preferences have changed over the years and why?'

In order to define more specifically those careers that might interest you, Part 2 from the previous section asked you to look at each area as a separate category. You should place your scores from each of the categories you completed in Part 2 in the charts that follow. Mark your score on each area with a tick, circle or cross, then join up the points. As with the test in Part 1, average scores will indicate careers about which you are more or less indifferent, low scores indicate careers you would probably undertake only on sufferance, whilst high scores indicate careers that you should consider.

You are most likely to have different interests in different categories. Comparing scores directly between categories may not give you an entirely valid result. This is because on one category you may have a high score because a type of work really did appeal to you more than all the others, whilst on another category you may get a high result because the type of work emerges as no more than the 'best of a bad bunch'. You have to interpret this information, using your common sense, realizing that equal scores on the graph do not necessarily imply equal importance.

To repeat what was stated earlier, it is true to say that any one career may fit as happily in one category as another. To put it another way, most careers require different bits of different categories in different proportions. It also depends upon the different orientation or purpose of the type of organization for which you may work. Furthermore, will the career you choose continue to retain the same satisfying aspects when you progress or gain promotion in the longer term? For example, if you find a career that satisfies your skills, perhaps with machinery, perhaps with people, will you be as happy if asked to take on more management responsibility or practise more administration?

Finally, you need to think through the implications your results on the aptitude and personality tests have for the career you pursue. With all this information at hand, look through the expanded list of careers within each category. With those that appeal, ask yourself how your aptitudes can assist you in being successful and how your strengths of personality may also work to your advantage.

# Category 1   Words or communication

| | | | | | | | | | |
|---|---|---|---|---|---|---|---|---|---|
| A | 0 | 1 | 2 | 3 | 4 | 5 | 6 | 7 | 8 |
| B | 0 | 1 | 2 | 3 | 4 | 5 | 6 | 7 | 8 |
| C | 0 | 1 | 2 | 3 | 4 | 5 | 6 | 7 | 8 |
| D | 0 | 1 | 2 | 3 | 4 | 5 | 6 | 7 | 8 |
| E | 0 | 1 | 2 | 3 | 4 | 5 | 6 | 7 | 8 |
| F | 0 | 1 | 2 | 3 | 4 | 5 | 6 | 7 | 8 |
| G | 0 | 1 | 2 | 3 | 4 | 5 | 6 | 7 | 8 |
| H | 0 | 1 | 2 | 3 | 4 | 5 | 6 | 7 | 8 |
| I | 0 | 1 | 2 | 3 | 4 | 5 | 6 | 7 | 8 |

A  journalism or writing
  – reporting, technical authorship, in-house or freelance, copy writing
B  publishing
  – editor, books, newspapers, periodicals, production control
C  museum exhibiting
  – art gallery, curator, keeper
D  library information
  – librarian, information officer, assistant, information science
E  archaeology
  – keeper, curator, fieldwork, writing, conservation, restoration
F  interpreting or translation
  – teaching, tourist guide, correspondent, courier, representative
G  acting
  – teacher, drama therapist, floor manager
H  broadcasting production/research
  – assistant, researcher, stage manager, sound technician, editor
I  legal advice
  – barrister, solicitor, clerk, executive

# Category 2   Music or art

| | | | | | | | | | | |
|---|---|---|---|---|---|---|---|---|---|---|
| A | 0 | 1 | 2 | 3 | 4 | 5 | 6 | 7 | 8 | 9 | 10 |
| B | 0 | 1 | 2 | 3 | 4 | 5 | 6 | 7 | 8 | 9 | 10 |
| C | 0 | 1 | 2 | 3 | 4 | 5 | 6 | 7 | 8 | 9 | 10 |
| D | 0 | 1 | 2 | 3 | 4 | 5 | 6 | 7 | 8 | 9 | 10 |
| E | 0 | 1 | 2 | 3 | 4 | 5 | 6 | 7 | 8 | 9 | 10 |
| F | 0 | 1 | 2 | 3 | 4 | 5 | 6 | 7 | 8 | 9 | 10 |
| G | 0 | 1 | 2 | 3 | 4 | 5 | 6 | 7 | 8 | 9 | 10 |
| H | 0 | 1 | 2 | 3 | 4 | 5 | 6 | 7 | 8 | 9 | 10 |
| I | 0 | 1 | 2 | 3 | 4 | 5 | 6 | 7 | 8 | 9 | 10 |
| J | 0 | 1 | 2 | 3 | 4 | 5 | 6 | 7 | 8 | 9 | 10 |
| K | 0 | 1 | 2 | 3 | 4 | 5 | 6 | 7 | 8 | 9 | 10 |

A   musician or music teacher
  – instrument technician, sound engineer
B   dancer
  – choreography, therapy, health and fitness, teaching
C   camera operator
  – special effects, lighting, mixing, editing
D   fashion model
  – dancing, beauty therapy
E   beautician or hairdresser
  – make-up artist, therapist
F   graphic designer or illustrator
  – graphics, 3-D, commercial, products, media, art direction
G   design of textiles or fashion
  – machining, cutting, industrial, craft
H   interior design
  – research, specifications, architecture, management, drafting, painting, decorating, window dressing
I   photography
  – medical, press, freelance, web design, imaging, film camera, artist
J   tailor or dressmaker
  – sewing, pattern cutter, examiner, dyeing, pressing, examiner, buying

K    upholsterer or polisher
   −    cabinet making, furniture design, boat building, antique
        restoration/conservation

## Category 3    Helping or teaching

| A | 0 | 1 | 2 | 3 | 4 | 5 | 6 | 7 | 8 | 9 | 10 | 11 |
|---|---|---|---|---|---|---|---|---|---|---|----|----|
| B | 0 | 1 | 2 | 3 | 4 | 5 | 6 | 7 | 8 | 9 | 10 | 11 |
| C | 0 | 1 | 2 | 3 | 4 | 5 | 6 | 7 | 8 | 9 | 10 | 11 |
| D | 0 | 1 | 2 | 3 | 4 | 5 | 6 | 7 | 8 | 9 | 10 | 11 |
| E | 0 | 1 | 2 | 3 | 4 | 5 | 6 | 7 | 8 | 9 | 10 | 11 |
| F | 0 | 1 | 2 | 3 | 4 | 5 | 6 | 7 | 8 | 9 | 10 | 11 |
| G | 0 | 1 | 2 | 3 | 4 | 5 | 6 | 7 | 8 | 9 | 10 | 11 |
| H | 0 | 1 | 2 | 3 | 4 | 5 | 6 | 7 | 8 | 9 | 10 | 11 |
| I | 0 | 1 | 2 | 3 | 4 | 5 | 6 | 7 | 8 | 9 | 10 | 11 |
| J | 0 | 1 | 2 | 3 | 4 | 5 | 6 | 7 | 8 | 9 | 10 | 11 |
| K | 0 | 1 | 2 | 3 | 4 | 5 | 6 | 7 | 8 | 9 | 10 | 11 |
| L | 0 | 1 | 2 | 3 | 4 | 5 | 6 | 7 | 8 | 9 | 10 | 11 |

A    personnel or training
   −    personnel, training officer, industrial relations, employee
        services, safety officer
B    nursing
   −    hospital, midwifery, district, health visitor, occupational
        health, nursing auxiliary/assistant
C    medical therapist or radiographer
   −    physiotherapist, radiographer, occupational therapist,
        chiropodist, speech or language therapist
D    complementary medicine
   −    osteopath, naturopath, medical herbalist, homeopath,
        acupuncturist, chiropractor, aromatherapist
E    social work
   −    field, residential, children, care assistant
F    probation work
   −    court work, prisons, after-care services, welfare

G  nursery or infant work
   – nursery nurse, infant teaching, class assistant, childminder, playgroup
H  employment or career work
   – recruitment, career officer – institutions or government
I  youth or community work
   – clubs, leisure centres, 'outreach worker', community affairs
J  psychology
   – clinical, educational, occupational, criminal, legal, psychotherapy, counselling
K  police or prison service
   – constabulary, mounted, criminal investigation, community liaison, prison officer, instruction, guard
L  teaching
   – schools – junior/senior – further education, welfare, indoor/outdoor, special needs, special support, class assistant

## *Category 4   Buying or selling*

| | | | | | | | |
|---|---|---|---|---|---|---|---|
| A | 0 | 1 | 2 | 3 | 4 | 5 | 6 | 7 |
| B | 0 | 1 | 2 | 3 | 4 | 5 | 6 | 7 |
| C | 0 | 1 | 2 | 3 | 4 | 5 | 6 | 7 |
| D | 0 | 1 | 2 | 3 | 4 | 5 | 6 | 7 |
| E | 0 | 1 | 2 | 3 | 4 | 5 | 6 | 7 |
| F | 0 | 1 | 2 | 3 | 4 | 5 | 6 | 7 |
| G | 0 | 1 | 2 | 3 | 4 | 5 | 6 | 7 |
| H | 0 | 1 | 2 | 3 | 4 | 5 | 6 | 7 |

A  marketing
   – management, research, promotions, import/export, pricing, product or category development
B  advertising
   – account management, planning, media
C  retail sales
D  public relations
E  travelling sales representative

F    buying or purchase agent
G    own business
H    shop franchise or public house
    –    licensee, franchisee, bar, restaurant, retail, hotel, club

# Category 5    Administration or accountancy

| | | | | | | | | | |
|---|---|---|---|---|---|---|---|---|---|
| A | 0 | 1 | 2 | 3 | 4 | 5 | 6 | 7 | 8 | 9 |
| B | 0 | 1 | 2 | 3 | 4 | 5 | 6 | 7 | 8 | 9 |
| C | 0 | 1 | 2 | 3 | 4 | 5 | 6 | 7 | 8 | 9 |
| D | 0 | 1 | 2 | 3 | 4 | 5 | 6 | 7 | 8 | 9 |
| E | 0 | 1 | 2 | 3 | 4 | 5 | 6 | 7 | 8 | 9 |
| F | 0 | 1 | 2 | 3 | 4 | 5 | 6 | 7 | 8 | 9 |
| G | 0 | 1 | 2 | 3 | 4 | 5 | 6 | 7 | 8 | 9 |
| H | 0 | 1 | 2 | 3 | 4 | 5 | 6 | 7 | 8 | 9 |
| I | 0 | 1 | 2 | 3 | 4 | 5 | 6 | 7 | 8 | 9 |
| J | 0 | 1 | 2 | 3 | 4 | 5 | 6 | 7 | 8 | 9 |

A    civil, local or health service
    –    administration officer/assistant, tax inspection, diplomatic
        service, medical records, computing, legal, company
        secretarial, purchasing and supply
B    post office work or secretarial
    –    operations, mail handling, personnel, information
        technology, private or executive secretary, reception, word
        processing
C    accounting or auditing
    –    costing, invoicing, wages, tax, insolvency, transactions,
        management, computer software, analysis
D    health and safety work
    –    trading standards, consumer affairs, customs,
        environment, legal enforcement, inspection and control
E    travel or tourism
    –    information centre, agency consultant, clerk, courier,
        representative, reception, passenger service, retail, tourism
        officer

F   legal executive or court services
- legal preparation and administration, management, probate, litigation, conveyancing, enquiry

G   banking or building society work
- clearing, merchant, investment, international, customer services, financial products – mortgages, investments, branch or specialist

H   insurance or stock exchange
- underwriting, broking, sales, claims official, clerk, surveyor, loss adjuster, market maker, stockbroker, investment analyst, trading, commodities, economist

I   housing management
- housing/estate officer/manager, renting, allocating, property administration

J   planning or surveying
- development, quantity, land, buildings, legislation, environmental factors, housing and economics, local authority, government, urban corporations, planning technician

## Category 6    Science or technology

| | | | | | | | | | | | |
|---|---|---|---|---|---|---|---|---|---|---|---|
| A | 0 | 1 | 2 | 3 | 4 | 5 | 6 | 7 | 8 | 9 | 10 | 11 |
| B | 0 | 1 | 2 | 3 | 4 | 5 | 6 | 7 | 8 | 9 | 10 | 11 |
| C | 0 | 1 | 2 | 3 | 4 | 5 | 6 | 7 | 8 | 9 | 10 | 11 |
| D | 0 | 1 | 2 | 3 | 4 | 5 | 6 | 7 | 8 | 9 | 10 | 11 |
| E | 0 | 1 | 2 | 3 | 4 | 5 | 6 | 7 | 8 | 9 | 10 | 11 |
| F | 0 | 1 | 2 | 3 | 4 | 5 | 6 | 7 | 8 | 9 | 10 | 11 |
| G | 0 | 1 | 2 | 3 | 4 | 5 | 6 | 7 | 8 | 9 | 10 | 11 |
| H | 0 | 1 | 2 | 3 | 4 | 5 | 6 | 7 | 8 | 9 | 10 | 11 |
| I | 0 | 1 | 2 | 3 | 4 | 5 | 6 | 7 | 8 | 9 | 10 | 11 |
| J | 0 | 1 | 2 | 3 | 4 | 5 | 6 | 7 | 8 | 9 | 10 | 11 |
| K | 0 | 1 | 2 | 3 | 4 | 5 | 6 | 7 | 8 | 9 | 10 | 11 |
| L | 0 | 1 | 2 | 3 | 4 | 5 | 6 | 7 | 8 | 9 | 10 | 11 |

A electronics or computer hardware
  - engineering, systems programming/analysis, service, applications
B software or web programming
  - software engineering, computer aided design, languages, business tools, information service, games
C environmental health
  - food, public health, disease, pollution, infection, inspector, health officer
D statistics or econometrics
  - statistician, economist, forecasting, modelling
E medicine or dentistry
  - general practice, hospital work, dentist, hygienist, technician
F pharmacy or chemistry
  - pharmacist or technician, pharmacologist, retail, laboratory analysis
G ophthalmic or medical technology
  - optometrist, ophthalmic optician, orthoptist, dispensing, medical technical officer, orthotics/prosthetics
H food science or dietetics
  - dietitian, home economist, food scientist, technologist, technician
I materials or earth sciences
  - metallurgist, materials scientist, geologist, meteorologist, oceanographer
J engineering
  - civil, mechanical, aeronautical, production, electrical, fabrication
K veterinary surgery
L pilot or air control
  - airline, engineer, controller

# Category 7  Activity or outdoors

| | | | | | | | | | | |
|---|---|---|---|---|---|---|---|---|---|---|
| A | 0 | 1 | 2 | 3 | 4 | 5 | 6 | 7 | 8 | 9 |
| B | 0 | 1 | 2 | 3 | 4 | 5 | 6 | 7 | 8 | 9 |
| C | 0 | 1 | 2 | 3 | 4 | 5 | 6 | 7 | 8 | 9 |
| D | 0 | 1 | 2 | 3 | 4 | 5 | 6 | 7 | 8 | 9 |
| E | 0 | 1 | 2 | 3 | 4 | 5 | 6 | 7 | 8 | 9 |
| F | 0 | 1 | 2 | 3 | 4 | 5 | 6 | 7 | 8 | 9 |
| G | 0 | 1 | 2 | 3 | 4 | 5 | 6 | 7 | 8 | 9 |
| H | 0 | 1 | 2 | 3 | 4 | 5 | 6 | 7 | 8 | 9 |
| I | 0 | 1 | 2 | 3 | 4 | 5 | 6 | 7 | 8 | 9 |
| J | 0 | 1 | 2 | 3 | 4 | 5 | 6 | 7 | 8 | 9 |

A  armed forces or security
   - army, navy, air force, police constable, private security, merchant navy
B  sport or leisure
   - coaching, instruction, sportsperson, sports management
C  bar, restaurant or kitchen work
   - catering, waiting, kitchen assistant, housekeeping
D  refuse, windows and cleaning
   - dry cleaning, laundry, window cleaning, refuse collection
E  ambulance or fire service
   - fire, coastguard, ambulance driving, control room
F  driving or traffic control
   - road, coach, bus, heavy goods, taxi, private hire, driving instruction, train driver, guard, line worker, fitter, technician
G  farm, horticulture or animal work
   - farm manager, worker, fish farming, plants, gardens, grounds person, veterinary nurse, animal welfare, groom, kennels, stables, riding instruction, zookeeper
H  forestry, parks or conservation
   - countryside conservation, warden, ranger, tree cutting
I  materials handling or funeral work
   - post, warehousing, lift truck and other equipment, undertaking
J  porter or hospital services
   - hospital porter, operating assistant

# Category 8   Manufacturing or construction

| | | | | | | | | |
|---|---|---|---|---|---|---|---|---|
| A | 0 | 1 | 2 | 3 | 4 | 5 | 6 | 7 |
| B | 0 | 1 | 2 | 3 | 4 | 5 | 6 | 7 |
| C | 0 | 1 | 2 | 3 | 4 | 5 | 6 | 7 |
| D | 0 | 1 | 2 | 3 | 4 | 5 | 6 | 7 |
| E | 0 | 1 | 2 | 3 | 4 | 5 | 6 | 7 |
| F | 0 | 1 | 2 | 3 | 4 | 5 | 6 | 7 |
| G | 0 | 1 | 2 | 3 | 4 | 5 | 6 | 7 |
| H | 0 | 1 | 2 | 3 | 4 | 5 | 6 | 7 |

A   using machines or manufacturing
  – craftsperson, operative
B   vehicle repair or maintenance
  – mechanic, auto electrician, body building and repair
C   telecoms or service engineering
  – electrician, technician, appliance technician, service engineering, welding
D   food preparation
  – baking, brewing, meat and other food process
E   making textiles or furniture
  – glass, leather, textiles, clothing, furniture
F   printing operations
  – compositing, scanning, machine printing, bookbinding, finishing
G   ironwork or building crafts
  – foundry, chemical plant, building trades – glazing, plumbing, plastering, roofing, scaffolding, tiling, flooring, painting and decorating
H   oil, highways and construction
  – drilling, roustabout, heavy machinery, plant operation

# Occupational Index

Scan through this list of professional careers, stopping where one appeals to you. Then there are three major questions to ask in relation to that career:

**1** How does it fit with my strengths or weaknesses of aptitude?

**2** Will I find it satisfying in view of my personality, particularly the approach I have to tasks and the way I relate to people?

**3** Does it accord with my interests and will it sustain my interest?

Then, you can find out more about each career from the careers section in your library in publications such as *Occupations*, published by COIC, or other publications by Kogan Page.

Astronaut
Astronomer
Auctioneer
Auditor
Author
Avionics engineer
Bacteriologist
Ballet dancer
Bank manager
Barperson/manager
Barrister
Beautician
Bespoke tailor
Bicycle repairer
Bilingual secretary
Biologist
Biomedical engineer
Book critic
Book editor
Book illustrator
Book publisher
Bookseller
Botanist
Brewer
Broker
Building demolition expert
Building inspector
Building society manager
Building surveyor
Bursar
Bus driver
Business consultant
Camera operator
Camera repairer
Car body designer
Car mechanic
Careers adviser

Cartographer
Cartoon animator
CD ROM producer
Chaplain
Chef
Chemical engineer
Chemical technologist
Chemist
Chief executive
Childcare worker
Children's nurse
Chiropodist
Chiropractor
Choreographer
Cinema manager
Civil engineer
Civil servant
Clinical psychologist
Clothing designer
Club manager
Coach driver
College admissions counsellor
Comic illustrator
Community social worker
Community warden
Company secretary
Computer animator
Computer game designer
Computer hardware engineer
Computer systems analyst
Confectioner
Conservation officer
Consumer research executive
Continuity supervisor
Copywriter
Coroner
Cost accountant

Health and safety inspector
Health services administrator
Health visitor
Heating engineer
Helicopter pilot
Herbalist
Historian
Home economist
Homeopath
Horologist
Horticulturalist
Hospital physicist
Hotel manager
Human resources manager
Hydrographic surveyor
Hydrologist
Illustrator
Immunologist
Importer/exporter
Industrial designer
Information officer
Information scientist
Instrument and control
   engineer
Instrument maker
Insurance adjuster
Interior designer
Interpreter
Jewellery maker
Journalist
Judge
Justices clerk
Landscape architect
Language teacher
Lawyer
Liberal studies teacher
Librarian

Linguist
Literary agent
Literary critic
Locomotive engineer
Loss adjuster
Management consultant
Managing director
Manufacturing engineer
Marine biologist
Marine engineer
Market researcher
Marketing manager
Materials scientist
Mathematician
Mechanical engineer
Medical illustrator
Medical photographer
Mental nurse
Merchandiser
Metallurgist
Meteorologist
Microbiologist
Microelectronics engineer
Midwife
Mining engineer
Minister of religion
Model maker
Music producer
Music therapist
Musician
Naturopath
Naval architect
Navigating officer
Neurosurgeon
Newspaper
   reporter/photographer
Notary public

Security officer
Service engineer/technician
Session musician
Set designer
Silversmith
Social scientist
Social worker
Software engineer
Solicitor
Sound engineer
Space salesperson
Speech therapist
Sports centre manager
Sports coach
Stage manager
Statistician
Stock controller
Stockbroker
Stonemason
Surgeon
Surveying technician
Surveyor
Systems analyst
Taxidermist
Teacher
Teacher of art/craft

Teacher of handicapped
Technical author
Technical illustrator
Technical representative
Technical writer
Telecommunications engineer
Textile designer
Theatre costume designer
Toolmaker
Town planning officer
Toymaker
Trading standards officer
Translator
Transport manager
Underwriter
Urban planner
Veterinary surgeon
Vision mixer
Vocational counsellor
Water engineer
Weather forecaster
Web master
Writer
Youth worker
Zookeeper
Zoologist

# Career Agenda Planner

To be successful in your career you will want to express all those factors of aptitude, personality and interests that you have explored in the foregoing sections. Hopefully, you will have discovered a theme that runs through all your test results. For example, if you are verbal, people oriented and have found that teaching appeals to you most, then your agenda will have a clear aim. Again, if you are visual and technical, have a precise, factual personality and find that science or computers interest you, there should be little difficulty in planning your career agenda. In cases like these, even though the direction may be clear, difficulty may still arise; often there are issues about how you actually get to where you want to be, or how you enable yourself to become what you want. Sometimes it is a question of obtaining the necessary qualifications, or of persuading others or of coping with issues that may arise when the career you want involves compromising your present way of life. Some of these matters are more acute for those who are already in a career because they are more likely to have ongoing commit-ments, often of a financial, social or geographical kind, that make career change a very big issue indeed, and often, not just for the individual concerned, but sometimes for the family of that person as well. I have known many, many people who have been bored in their work and have stayed with it for many years for fear of risking a style of life to which they and their family had been accustomed.

In my experience of advising many thousands of people about their career there have been very few occasions when someone has thought 'Eureka!' upon discovering a wonderful career that has never occurred to them before, but promises to be the answer to everything. It does happen, but rarely. For most people, career planning is a gradual adjustment because it is almost always a matter of balancing various elements in life that are connected with such a major decision as to what one is going to do during most days of one's life. It is easier if you are young, because you are more likely to be a free agent. For older people who may have been working for some time, there are often commitments that can create conflict because although those commitments have been freely entered into and are often desirable in themselves, they can also lead to a feeling of entrapment. At the same time, my experience is that there is always scope for adjustment and refocusing in every career. No doubt you can find a way that leads to career fulfilment. If radical change is impossible, such as a completely new career, then embark on small changes that provide more of the qualitative factors that will make you feel you are getting where you want. This is why it is a good idea to write down your agenda because you will have a reference and can more objectively check your progress, thus ensuring that you pursue your strategy and achieve your objective.

## My present career situation

Use the evidence and suggestions from Part 1 together with your own evaluation. Write down some key and meaningful words that describe your situation.

### Part 1   Aptitudes

| My aptitudes are: | How much are my aptitudes used appropriately: | Career(s) in which I could use my aptitudes: |
| --- | --- | --- |
| _____ | _____ | _____ |
| _____ | _____ | _____ |
| _____ | _____ | _____ |
| _____ | _____ | _____ |

### Part 2   Personality

| My personality is: | How effectively am I expressing my personality: | Career(s) in which I could express my personality: |
| --- | --- | --- |
| _____ | _____ | _____ |
| _____ | _____ | _____ |
| _____ | _____ | _____ |
| _____ | _____ | _____ |

## Part 3   Career analysis

| My interests are: | How much are my interests satisfied: | Career(s) that would satisfy my interests: |
|---|---|---|
| _____ | _____ | _____ |
| _____ | _____ | _____ |
| _____ | _____ | _____ |
| _____ | _____ | _____ |

From what you have written in the right-hand column you distil the overall best career(s) to pursue. It may be that you are doing it already, in which case this exercise will have been worthwhile as a 'quality check'. But where there are discrepancies between the middle column and the right-hand column these will be matters for career agenda planning.

**Overall most suitable career(s)**

_____

_____

**Timescale in which to obtain this career**

_____

# My future career situation

In the following instances write about yourself in the future and tick the point on the dimension to indicate how far you have attained what you want:

**How I will feel about myself in this career**

**How I will look**

_____

_____

**Poor   0   1   2   3   4   5   6   7   8   9   10   Excellent**

**What I will own**

_____

_____

**Not much   0   1   2   3   4   5   6   7   8   9   10   A lot**

**How I think and feel about myself**

_____

_____

**Poor   0   1   2   3   4   5   6   7   8   9   10   Excellent**

**What people think and feel about me**

_____

_____

**Poor   0   1   2   3   4   5   6   7   8   9   10   Excellent**

**I describe my career using these words**

_____

_____

**Poor   0   1   2   3   4   5   6   7   8   9   10   Excellent**

Taking the career that is most suitable, what do you need to change in order to obtain it? Even if these areas are not necessarily areas of difficulty it is worth making a statement as to your situation. Be specific about any issues or difficulties that may prevent you getting what you want.

**1  Health**

_____

_____

How I will overcome any health issues

_____

_____

## 2 Circumstances

_____

_____

How I will cope with circumstances that are unfavourable

_____

_____

## 3 Education

_____

_____

How I will obtain any education necessary

_____

_____

## 4 Age/experience

_____

_____

How I will obtain the experience that will qualify me

_____

_____

## 5 Commitments

_____

_____

What I will do in order not to be limited

_____

_____

## 6 Risks

_____

_____

How I will limit or address risks

_____

_____

## 7  Other

_____

_____

How I will overcome any other conflicts/difficulties

_____

_____

As well as attempting to realize one's own talents, as if that were not difficult enough, it is often the case that you will want to involve other people who may be affected by what you want to do. Indeed, to the extent that what you do touches their lives they may also want to feel confident about what you may do. Do not dismiss, ignore or hide from any concerns they may have. Think carefully about how to involve them.

**People I need to involve**

_____

_____

_____

_____

**What they may say about what I want to do**

_____

_____

_____

_____

**What I will say in response**

_____

_____

_____

_____

Make a list of specific actions you will take in relation to your career agenda. Place a tick at the left-hand side upon completion.

**1 Today or tomorrow**

✓ _____

_____

_____

**2 By next week**

_____

_____

_____

**3 Longer term**

_____

_____

_____

**Next date I will read through and check my career agenda**

_____

# Bibliography

*Aptitude, Personality and Motivation Tests*, Third edition, Jim Barrett, Kogan Page, 2009

*The Aptitude Test Workbook*, Revised edition, Jim Barrett, Kogan Page, 2008

*Career, Aptitude and Selection Tests*, Third edition, Jim Barrett, Kogan Page, 2009

*How to Administer & Interpret Psychometric Tests*, Jim Barrett, Psychometrictests.com, 2001

*Test Your Numerical Aptitude*, Jim Barrett, Kogan Page, 2007

*Test Your Own Aptitude*, Third edition, Jim Barrett and Geoff Williams, Kogan Page, 2003

*Total Leadership*, Jim Barrett, Kogan Page, 1999

With over 1,000 titles in printed and digital format, **Kogan Page** offers affordable, sound business advice

**www.koganpage.com**

**KoganPage**